WITHOUT RESERVATION

THE RIBALD MEMOIRS OF
FAMOUS HOTELIER

ALAN TREMAIN

the Peppertree Press
Sarasota, Florida

For information regarding permission,
call 941-922-2662 or contact us at our website:
www.peppertreepublishing.com or write to:
the Peppertree Press, LLC.
Attention: Publisher
1269 First Street, Suite 7
Sarasota, Florida 34236

ISBN: 978-1-936051-78-6
Library of Congress Number: 2009944190

Printed in the U.S.A.
Printed February 2010

List of Chapters

CHAPTER ONE

Mobknobbing at the Copley Plaza

M obsters, like anyone else, love parties. But, unlike most others, they do it bigger and better and what is more, they can afford it and they pay cash. My secretary, Linda, buzzed me on the intercom and told me there was someone that wanted to put on, as he called it, a big bash. Linda said, "He wouldn't give me his name and he sounds nasty and tough and he insists on speaking to you personally." I said, "Sure, put him through." I picked up the phone and was greeted with, "Hey Mister T, I've got an anniversary coming up and I want to throw a great bash for about 300 people." Somewhere along the way, because I had arranged so many weddings and functions for the Italian community I had earned the honorary title, at least in the north end of Boston, of "Mr. T." Linda was right, and I cannot even start to describe his voice, but he sounded right out of a B grade gangster movie. He continued, "How much is it going to cost me?" I said, "Well, that depends on what type of menu you have, music, etc., etc." "OK," he said, "I'll be up to see you tomorrow afternoon at 3 p.m., OK." I looked quickly at my Brooks Brothers Diary and said, "Sure, that is just fine." Then I added, "By the way, who am I speaking to?" He answered, "Hey Mr. T. just call me Larry and I'll see you tomorrow at 3 p.m." Mind you, I was really not that surprised. We did a tremendous number of functions for the Italian community and a lot of fathers and grooms not only sound, but also look like the actor Edward G. Robinson, who was the typecast gangster in movies 20 years ago.

Sure enough the next afternoon, looking like his voice, Larry turns up at my office. He was about 5'8", probably 250 pounds, in other words, very heavy. He wore a three-piece dark suit, white shirt, yellow tie, French cuffs, and an expensive pair of gold and diamond cuff links, highly polished shoes, a black cashmere overcoat and a black Derby hat. The whole outfit was topped off with the proverbial diamond ring on the pinkie. I decided to give him the part of the Godfather, not Marlon Brando. Following in his footsteps were two goons, to use a bit of gangster terminology that was current. One with an alligator briefcase, to make him look more businesslike.

Larry said, "I like your office, Mr. T." and started to wander around looking at everything. It is true, it was a great office and I had furnished it to look like what the Copley Plaza probably looked like back in 1912. A big French Ormolu desk, oriental carpets and lots of antiques. Larry said, "Nice place you got here." I sort of thought I had heard that somewhere before. He added, "But you got lots of class Mr. T. and that's why my friends get married in this hotel." As I said before, he was right. A lot of them did.

I suggested they all be seated, which Larry did, but not his henchmen. They played the part to the hilt and stood over by the door looking around the room. Larry wanted to invite between 250 to 300 people so I suggested the Venetian Room and the Oval Room. Two great rooms. The Oval Room was probably one of the most magnificent rooms to have a function on the east coast of the United States. It held 300 and, as the name implies, it is oval, with a magnificently painted cloud ceiling and gold and plaster baroque. Where the band or the orchestra plays from is an enormous, sort of 1920's shell, which always gives a great backdrop to the band and the singers. The other room, the Venetian Room, is off the Oval Room and is used for cocktail receptions. It is also a magnificent room of white and gold mirror and marble and the two combined are probably the most beautiful rooms to either get married in or have a special function, certainly in Boston. He accepted my recommendations and said, "You got a deal." I asked Linda to check if they were available on the evening that he wanted and luckily enough they were. I asked Larry what he had in mind. He said, "Eh, Mr. T., I want a slap-up dinner. The best wines, cigars, liquor, the best that the house can provide. I want 'the works'. Good music and I want everybody to be happy. So, what's it gonna' cost me?" I said, "Well, let's talk about the menu." He said, "Eh, Mr. T., you take care of it. You're the expert; just tell me what it's going to cost." I started to mumble about open bars and good wines and dinner, etc., and I said, "Well, probably around $150 a head." He thought for a moment and he said, "That's a lot of bread." I replied, "You told me you wanted the best and you picked the best hotel. We are a union hotel and that costs money and we buy the best produce." He said, "Yeah, those unions, they're a pain in the ass." He added, "OK, Mr. T., you got a deal." He turned to one of his henchman and said, "Give the man thirty thousand dollars." The goon puts the briefcase on my desk, opens it up and it's full of money and he starts putting bundles on my desk. I couldn't believe it. After covering half of my desk with cash, the guy said, "OK, you got thirty thousand dollars."

I might add that there was at least two thirds of the briefcase still full of money. I said, "Thank you very much; I need to have someone count it and of course give you a receipt." I buzzed Linda to have someone from the comptroller's office come over. At which point Larry seemed to get quite upset and said, "Hey, Mr. T., what's the problem, don't you trust me? I'll tell you what, if it's a dollar short I'll give you a thousand bucks for every dollar I am short and you can put it in your own pocket." "That's fine Larry," I said, "but I have to account for it and I presume you want a receipt." To which he replied, "A receipt! Come on. I just want a great party and I'll see you in five weeks." He got up and left my office. Linda graciously gave them their coats. Larry put on his, at which time he tried to pinch Linda's behind, gave a big laugh and said, "Bye, everybody." Linda said to me, "Who was that?" "Well," I said, "that was Larry, a very well known character around Boston. I think we had getter get John Cronis and everyone over from the catering office and make sure that we set up a spectacular party."

Jim D'Angelo, the comptroller, arrived with an assistant and started to count the money. He sent the assistant over to the bank at one point, just to make sure that it wasn't counterfeit, since most of it was 5's, 10's and 20's. Believe me $30,000 is a lot of cash in small bills. But Larry was right. It was there to the dollar. I then called over Cronis, the director of Catering. We made out the menus, called our Director of Special Events to get involved and make sure the room would look spectacular with lots of flowers and decorations. We booked a twelve-piece band, a Tony Bennett type singer, finalized all the costs. I then made a note in my diary to check everything out on the day of the function.

Some weeks later, one afternoon after returning from lunch, Bill, the Resident Manager walked into my office, quietly closing the door behind him and said, "Sir, we have a real problem." I said, "What's that Bill?" He said, "We have a meeting of the Mafia here tonight." Suddenly I remembered the famed anniversary party. "What makes you think it's a Mafia party?" I asked. He responded, "Because I've

4

had the FBI and some people from Interpol in my office most of the afternoon." I looked at him and said, "What on earth do they want?" He said, "Well, they think that every Mafia boss has been invited from the east coast, from Providence, Philadelphia, New York, New Jersey, etc., etc., and they want to take a picture of everyone who is attending the function tonight." He added, "I agreed rather reluctantly to let them take pictures from my office." Bill's office was located off of mine and bridged the lobby. From his window and his desk you could see anyone who entered the lobby and the elevators and from any one of the entrances. I looked at him a little askance and exclaimed in a slightly higher pitched voice that usual, "You did what, Bill?! You're crazy! First of all, we will never get another Italian wedding or function in this hotel. Secondly, they will probably blow the place up tomorrow and seriously, it is an invasion of privacy of our guests. For Christ sake, go back and tell these guys that there is no way that they can take pictures from your office or from inside the hotel." Bill looked at me crestfallen and said, "You've got to be kidding! It's the FBI and Interpol and they are not very pleasant." He added, "Why don't you come and talk to them." So I went into Bill's office and here was sitting three or four well dressed young men, two with hearing aids, which I later realized were communications earphones and they started to talk in cliché's about criminals and the Mafia and our responsibility to help them. They too, sounded like something out of a B-grade movie.

I said, "Gentlemen, these people are guests in our hotel and there is no way that you are going to invade their privacy. I am sorry but you cannot take pictures from our hotel. You will have to do something from the outside." Well, did that ever open a can of worms. They all got up and said threateningly, "You'll be hearing from us."

I started getting phone calls from all over the place. The FBI, Washington, the State Department. Finally I called my friend, Ed Masterman, who is also our corporate lawyer and explained to him what the situation was. I said, "I am not only getting phone calls, but they are threatening me because I refuse to let the FBI take pictures from inside the hotel." I explained that I had just received a threatening call from Washington from a Mr. Sullivan. Ed immediately interjected and said, "My God, that's the Chief Justice. What did he want?" I replied, "He told me that I had some of the most dangerous criminals in the world coming to my hotel and that I was obstructing justice." I said to Ed that I wasn't very diplomatic and that I said, "If they are the most dangerous criminals in the world, why aren't they in jail. Why are they in my hotel?" To which he suggested that I was being a smart ass to which I suggested that I was just an English country boy and I didn't know anything about the Mafia. As far as I was concerned, no one was going to come into the hotel and take pictures. Ed said, "Well, you've got a problem, but you are quite right. I don't think you should let the authorities come in the hotel. I will make some calls. Many phone calls later, Ed had convinced them to set up cameras and vans outside the hotel.

I was now starting to get a little nervous about the function and decided that I better keep a close watch on it and decided to be on hand that evening when the function started and make sure that at least the hotel did their job properly. Sure enough that evening around seven o'clock the Lincoln's and Cadillac's started to pull up outside the hotel. I had never seen so many large black cars with tinted windows and telephone aerials in my life. And the guests that were arriving in to the Oval Room were really unbelievable. Naturally, all the men wore dinner jackets, though not exactly Brooks Brothers, and all the dollies, because that's really what they were, wore mink coats and other expensive furs and had blonde beehive hairdos that I thought went out of style in the 50's. It was a fascinating group of characters and my partner, Jean-Claude Mathot, who was managing one of our other hotels in Providence, Rhode Island, joined me. He said, "Boy, a lot of these people look very familiar."

We walked around to the Venetian Room, which was where the

function was to start with cocktails. I had forgotten that they had requested a coat check room with special instruction that they could have put one of their own people in the check room, as they said, because they wanted to check their guest's expensive furs, since we normally didn't do that and they would be responsible for them. What we were amazed to find out was that they were also checking all types and styles of guns, putting labels on them and hanging them on a board out of the public's eye. I decided that this function was getting a little out of hand, but decided that discretion was the better part of valor. It seemed that they had their own security well in hand. It seemed quite a formal party. At least there was a receiving line and everyone was going through paying his or her respects to Larry and some other obvious VIP's.

The Boston Herald reported the next day that the FBI commented it was a repeat of the 1957 meeting of the mob at the Appalachia New York home of Joe Barbara. Jean-Claude and I decided to walk through the Venetian and Oval Room to check out the function and see that all was going well, and indeed, everything seemed to be in full swing. Everyone was enjoying themselves. As I had previously stated, it was black tie, except that most had removed their black ties and jackets and it was really rather hilarious because the men were sitting around with holsters strapped on and of course no firearms in them.

Meanwhile, the FBI was supposedly outside hidden in vans, video taping the arrival of the guests. It was like a low budget Hollywood premiere. In their unrelenting effort to photograph the "March of the Mafia," the FBI had failed to inform the Boston police of the gala event. And while the mob was mob knobbing, Boston's finest were having a big bash, down the street at the Dorothy Quinsy Suite, in the old Hancock building, honoring a retiree, with a three course chicken dinner at eight dollars a head. Somewhere between their entrée and dessert, word got to the police that a plot was afoot and things moved from "Operation Appalachia Copley Plaza" to "Operation Keystone

Cops." The Police Commissioner retiring to a back room with his top aides called a war commission. The question: how to deal a crushing blow to the mob. Then, minutes later, action. Copley Square soon looked like the Southeast Expressway at commuter time with a traffic accident thrown in as a bonus. Flashing lights, sirens, cameras, action! The Grand Dame was under siege. Boston's finest had come in force, in tow trucks to be exact, to tow away the double-parked beauties of Detroit. Evidently, the only legal remedy that could be found. The doorman who had been tossed the keys by every hood in the country and told "take care of it," was having a blue fit. Soon, the word spread throughout the Oval Room about the dirty work going on outside. It didn't seem to bother anyone. They kept right on dancing with their ladies and holsters and the local Tony Bennet kept right on singing that he lost his heart in San Francisco.

I went to discuss the events outside with Larry and to assure him that I could do nothing about the spectacle outside. Smiling, he said, "Listen, Mr. T., these are the uncertainties in life, right?" "Right," I said. He then told me to let the cops have their fun and before the night was over they'd get bored. He added, "Just order me a dozen limousines so that my guests can use them if they need them." He then got up and made a little speech. "Unless you have something in your trunk which might reveal trade secrets," he said with a few laughs, "don't be concerned."

Three guys nearly killed themselves trying to get to the door. Twelve limousines were confirmed. "Yup, you got it Mr. T.," said Larry. "As they tow our stuff away the boys will go down to the pound in the limos, pay the fine, among other things, bring back the cars and double park them again. We'll do it all night if we have to until they bring back the whole lot. I never met a towing stiff who couldn't be had; they love the smell of ready cash. One other thing Mr. T., keep things going until the cops are under control, and believe me they will be. Nothing stops. Plenty of champagne for the ladies, keep the boys happy with the booze. That's the way it is with us, business as usual, and Mr. T., run a tab for the limos, etc. I'll be around to see you in a couple of days."

"No problem sir," I answered. It worked just as the great prophet Larry said. The cops threw in the sponge after going back and forth to the pound most of the night each time increasing their take. I was told later that a good deal of cash changed hands that night and some of Boston's finest went home nearly as happy as Larry's guests. The FBI put me on their shit list, but I felt more comfortable on theirs than on Larry's, which is certainly where I would have been, had I let the FBI into the hotel and he found out about it.

I considered the whole history until several days later when Larry and one of his strong silent types showed up. He's come to settle the additional several thousand dollars owed. His man carried the cash in a brown paper bag. Jimmy took out the money and put it on the table. "Great party," he said.

"You want to count it again?" "No thanks," I said, "I have absolute faith in your accounting."

"I bet you say that to all the guys." Now that the amenities were out of the way I wanted to say my goodbyes to Larry, but he said that there was a little business that must be settled before he left.

Oh God, I thought. It's got to have something to do with the parking. He's probably going to tell me I'd need protection and I should pay to keep the police off my back, which is what I understand some of the restaurants have to do in the North End. "Business Larry? Tell me, what is it? I'll see what I can do for you."

"My mother, she tore her dress on one of your chairs at the party." Christ, I thought this is going to cost me a small fortune. Momma must have certainly been decked out in her most expensive Yves St. Laurent or Courrages dress or something equally exotic. Putting on my most persuasive English accent, which Larry kept on telling me he liked, I explained that as much as I understood his mother's distress, this was really an insurance problem and not my responsibility and that I'd be happy to file a claim for him.

"Fuck you Mr. T., fuck your insurance company. I only care about my Momma's dress and you'd better fucking buy her a new one." I couldn't believe how excited he had suddenly become. Preparing myself for the worst I asked what he had in mind, hoping he would spare my pain by a quick bullet.

"I just want the same dress like this one, no more, no less." He reached into the shopping bag and took out Momma's torn dress. "Ok what's right is right, right?" "Right", I said.

"You, Mr. T., or whoever, has got to go down to Filene's basement and buy my mother another one of these dresses and send it to her with a nice note of apology. They're on sale for $69.95 so you better hurry."

Jesus Christ, I almost kissed my first Mafioso, which I'm sure would have been my last!

"No problem," I said and started taking $70 from his cash and then ask Linda to take a taxi to Filene's and buy another dress and have someone from the Concierge department to drop it over to his mother's house.

"Don't put a finger on that money," Larry almost shouted. "I want your money, the Copley's money, your fucking management's money. I want you to go to your cashier and take out your money, and then send who the fuck it is to Feline's and buy a dress for my Momma so that she'll get the hell off my back! OK, Mr. T?"

"OK, Larry, I will take care of everything." He looked at me, having calmed down and said, "OK, OK, Mr. T, great party," and left.

I couldn't understand why he got so excited and why it was so important to pay him from the hotel's money, and then I became a little worried that his was counterfeit. I called the comptroller on the phone and said, "You'd better come over and pick this money up and take it over to the bank and have it checked.

It was the real thing.

CHAPTER TWO

British Public School

George Bernard Shaw, who detested the British Public School System addressed my class at Sevenoaks, a public school in the heart of Kent, and informed us that youth was wasted on the young and that real life was passing us by while we were cloistered in an anachronism. I was later to prove him wrong.

It was the start of my love of the good life.

My father was determined that I should attend a fine school and become a refined gentleman. For me, attending Sevenoaks was a strenuous pursuit of discomfort at extraordinarily expensive fees. The school was a forbidding stone building built in 1418. I believe it had the original beds, it certainly felt like it. It was very strict. You had to wear a grey suit, black tie, straw boater hat and black shoes. On Sundays you attended church at least twice, in the morning and evening. You were not allowed to run at any time. You walked everywhere like a gentleman. Under no circumstances could you ever leave the school grounds during the school term except one Sunday a month when your parents were allowed to come and pick you up to take you out for lunch.

The school stood in the shadows of a very famous English mansion called Knoll House, home of the infamous Sacksville West family, a family that would later on give me my first insight into the aristocracy of Great Britain.

Sevenoaks was ruled over by a pompous old codger named Higgs-Walker. He was a historian and was the head master. There was also a Mrs. Higgs-Walker whose voice was not only superlatively resonant, but had a bark to it much like a sea lion in heat.

Mrs. Higgs-Walker surrounded herself with a group of young boys who were called "fags", no relation to today's interpretation. They were a specially chosen group of boys who would run errands to the village and take her small Pekinese dog, "Poppit" for a walk. I was soon to realize that taking the dog for a walk and running errands gave you the opportunity to escape into the outer world, so my first challenge was to become one of these privileged "fags." I decided that since the dog was very small and obviously walked slowly, the best opportunity for staying out of the school for any length of time was to become Poppit's official walker. So, I went to the school library, swatted up on Pekinese dogs and became an instant expert. At the first opportunity I expounded my great newfound knowledge on Mrs. Higgs-Walker who quickly became impressed with my knowledge of her small dog. Shortly thereafter, I was ensconced in her entourage and named Chief Dog Walker. I was a fair half-miler and soon discovered that if I picked Poppit up and tucked her under my arm like a relay baton, I could make the village, buy the odd bottle of cheap sherry or dirty magazine to conduct a little black-marketing back in the dormitory. This quickly became quite a profit center.

On one of my visits into the village, I noticed a very charming inn called The White Hart and decided that when my father asked me where I wanted to go for lunch on his next visit, I would suggest this inn. I had heard that it not only had great food, but one of the retired chefs from Claridges Hotel in London was now its head chef. I thought it would be an interesting place to go.

Two Sundays later my father did, in fact, pick me up for lunch. We went to the White Hart Inn and during the course of lunch I suggested to the Maitre d' that I would like to visit the kitchen much like a young boy asks to see the cockpit in an airplane. I was duly introduced to the chef who was very flattered that a young man from "Sevenoaks" was interested in his kitchen and his food, and I truly was. From then on when I had the opportunity, it was an easy matter for me to quick march Poppit into the village and chat with the chef. I was genuinely fascinated in what was created in the kitchen and the chef really seemed to take a liking to me. One day around 2:30 in the afternoon, he had almost finished serving his Sunday crowd and asked me if I would like to join him in the corner of the kitchen to taste some of the delicious veal and ham pie that he had made that day, followed by a wonderful blackberry flan that he proceeded to sprinkle with sherry. It was one of the best meals that I had ever had.

Much to my surprise I was in for yet another great experience. It turns out that the Governor, that's what the owner of the inn was called, had a very pretty daughter around 15 or 16. One day when I was chatting with chef, she came wandering into the kitchen looking for something to eat. The chef introduced me explaining my culinary interest. She then asked me if I would like to visit the front of the house and see the dining room. I explained to her, that I had had lunch there, but I would love a tour of the hotel. Her name was Brenda and she introduced me to her father who thought that it was wonderful that his daughter was hobnobbing with someone from such an institution as Sevenoaks school and soon I was sitting down at a table with Brenda enjoying a wonderful selection from the menu and even the odd glass of good claret, passed surreptitiously to me by the Maitre d'. Life was really looking up and Poppit's walks were getting longer and longer.

A couple of weeks later on a Saturday night, I was to explore yet another side of the hospitality business. Sevenoaks School stood on the grounds of the famous Knoll House, which was an English manor set in a richly wooded park of several hundred acres, populated with deer and other game. The Sacksville West family who were in residence at the time did a lot of entertaining and on occasion, several boys would be chosen to go up to the manor on a Saturday evening to act as sort of pages who collected coats. On one particular occasion I was indeed to be one of the lucky few. The Sacksville Wests have been called wise and foolish, virtuous and wicked, but never dull. The Knoll House goes back to 1281, a huge castle type building with 12 chimneys. One for every month of the year. Seven courtyards, one for every day of the week, 52 staircases and 365 rooms. I have no idea why. According to history, it was the hand of the Archbishop of Canterbury. It is said that Thomas More (the Man for all Seasons) was a resident until Henry the VIII claimed it from the church. It stayed in the Royal Family until Queen Elizabeth in 1586 gave it to her cousin, Thomas Sacksville, who promptly ensconced his mistress there. I believe the mistress was the grandmother of the famous author Victoria Sacksville West. The mistress's name was Pappita. There was a marvelous reclining nude of her in one of the entrance halls and I used to caress her behind whenever I was lucky enough to work there. It always seemed to give me promise of what was perhaps to become a good omen.

Most of the time the functions were in the ballroom which was a magnificent, unbelievably luxuriously furnished room. It had a huge marble fireplace going from floor to ceiling with a coat of arms carved into it. Other times the parties were in the billiard room where the tables, balls and cues were reputably those of Charles the First. Whenever possible, I used to have a game of snooker if I arrived early enough, so that I could say that I played with Charles the First's balls!

My first visit turned out to be my first look at British aristocracy. It was a marvelous dinner served by white-gloved waiters and a wonderful sommelier with chains around his neck that generously poured what I understood to be a rare and exotic wine. My job throughout the evening was to simply take coats as people entered and then after dinner to pass around cigars and a cigar cutter. I had several lectures from those in attendance on what was and was not a good cigar. The men retired to the study to enjoy a port and the cigars, and the ladies went off to chatter in the drawing room. I, along with the other boys, went to the kitchen and helped us to a rather nice dinner from the leftovers and even a little cheese and a small glass of port. As the butler led us out to a car to return us to the school house I could not resist caressing the behind of the reclining nude, once again thinking that my future life looked quite promising.

Admittedly, academically I was not doing very well at school. Educationally, however, I was learning a lot. During the school holidays, I went to Bognor Regis where my aunties operated a very small private hotel on the waterfront. It seemed apparent that I was becoming interested in the art of inn keeping but I was always glad to get back to school and back to Brenda and the White Hart Inn. It appeared that we had a lot in common. I was a hungry young man who liked good food and she was the lovely daughter of the innkeeper.

The Higgs-Walkers left for visits with friends and lunches that often lasted 2 or 3 hours on which occasions Poppit was left with me. Sunday lunches at the White Hart were becoming quite ceremonious. Brenda and I were routinely ushered to a little corner table by the fireplace in the dining room and the waiters and the maitre d' would really fuss over us. Even Poppit enjoyed sitting in front of the fire. In fact it got to be so enjoyable that I used to suggest to my father that, although I enjoyed immensely his visits once a month, to take me out of this horrible boarding school, I really had to study extremely hard for exams and asked that he please forgive me for not being able to join him on this or that particular Sunday. Of course he thought it was the ultimate sacrifice that I should stay to study. He was delighted that I had finally taken to the academic life and hoped that I would soon by a budding lawyer or a doctor. Little did he know that I was spending a couple of hours in comparative luxury with a beautiful young lady at the local hostelry. My relationship with Brenda, in fact, was becoming really most interesting extending beyond the joys of food and wine. On a couple of occasions, Mrs. Higgs-Walker was a little suspicious that I was away so long with her dog, but I explained that we often sat and watched rabbits and the deer in the park and got a little carried away. She thought that was very charming.

It's a strange and terrible thing, but for some unfair reason all good things come to an end. One Sunday I arrived at the White Hart to find Brenda's parents away. She said that if I would like to spend a little more time than usual I could do so. Brenda and I and of course Poppit quietly slipped into her parents apartment, which was a Victorian, two-bedroom apartment with those wonderful lead light windows that looked out onto the marvelous green countryside of Sevenoaks. I must say the bedroom was very quaint and on the bed was one of those huge overstuffed eiderdown. We quickly got undressed, dove into the eiderdown and discovered what went well with food and wine. Since we didn't have that much time, after about 20 minutes, we got dressed and went down to the dining room. By this time, I was starved. So we let Poppit run in the garden while Brenda and I had a wonderful roast beef and Yorkshire pudding luncheon with a delightful bottle of 1913 claret, seated in the booth beside the fireplace.

Unbeknown to me a drama of great consequences was about to unfold. One that, as they say, would change the course of history, at least mine.

Mrs. Higgs-Walker, along with two of her most boring friends decided to take the Rolls out for a spin and stop for a spot of lunch at their favorite Inn. They approached their picturesque and historic landmark and were suddenly shocked out of their tranquility by the sight of poor little Poppit running around the garden. After rescuing Poppit and putting her safely in the back of the Rolls with a bowl of cold water, the rest of the party calmed Mrs. Higgs-Walker with a shot or two of sherry in the private lounge. They decided to proceed with lunch while someone tried to find where I was and what on earth the dog was doing at the White Hart.

Unfortunately this little incident was about to seriously cramp my style. They were seated right next to a delightful twosome. Suddenly we made eye contact and I don't know who was the more surprised. Mrs. Higgs-Walker got very excited muttering about her little Poppit. I know that I never got to finish my second glass of claret. Nor, for that matter, did I finish my education at Sevenoaks.

Unfortunately, I was already under a suspension threat since I had been caught raiding the Irish maid's quarters at 2 a.m. in the morning, only a week before. Knowing my fate I decided it was almost not worth going back to school, but I didn't have any money with me and I had to go to my locker to pick up my clothes. While planning an elegant retreat, I was detained when I got back to the school and unceremoniously delivered to the study of the Headmaster. Mr. Higgs-Walker then proceeded, in front of his wife, to tell me that I was the most unsavory character, obviously bent on living a scurrilous life and under no circumstances would I be allowed to stay and influence the lives of the unsuspecting boys around me that came from unblemished homes. I thought he was really very eloquent and actually agreed with him. Miraculously, I had just passed my matriculation, so at least I had the basis of an education. I really couldn't see the point of another three years of unadulterated boredom. So, to the cheering of a few of my friends, I left Sevenoaks School before the end of the term. My father was most annoyed with the whole incident. He thought the

Alan Tremain, aged 16, a chef trainee (or commis as the position was called in those days) in his first job at Browns Hotel in London.

school was terribly stuffy and most unreasonable. I explained that it was really because of the dog that I got expelled, not the women, nor the food and wine and actually I think he was quite relieved that he did not have to go on paying those exorbitant fees.

As a sort of epilogue of my informative years, I never quite knew who led whom astray. It turns out that Brenda was studying to be a ballet dancer. Her father, when he found out the sort of scandal that she had been part of, sent her off to study at Sadlers Wells in London. I understand she became a very talented student. However, some four or five years later when my mother and father were attending a convention in the city of Brussels, my father saw on a billboard what appeared to be a picture of Brenda. She was performing that night. Her name was not listed as the Brenda Biggs that I had known. She was now BB Champagne, the famous stripper from Paris. My father was intrigued enough to go into the nightclub to see if it really was Brenda and sure enough it was. Not only was she a stripper, but also she was the mistress of a Belgian gangster. Obviously, she too had seen the light and headed from Sevenoaks to the better life. Interestingly enough, many years later in 1961, when I was visiting my parents and we were discussing Brenda, my father informed me that she had, a few years earlier, returned to the little charming village of Chislehurst, Kent. According to the locals she had returned from abroad after studying classical dance. She then married the local Lloyds Bank Manager. I tried to call her to talk over old times and still see if we had something in common, but unfortunately missed her and time did not permit a second chance.

CHAPTER THREE

What Do You Mean, A Job?

Obviously now, at the early age of 16, I had to get a job and try to support myself. My father was not at all thrilled when I suggested that I was going to try to get a job in a hotel, but with a fatherly shrug he said, "Well, do as you please." In any case it was not going to be easy. I was very young to get a job in a hotel. I had no formal education in the hotel business, such as a recognized hotel school, but I really wanted to start in the kitchen. I liked the informal, creative atmosphere. It was part of a real excitement. Upstairs everyone was far too formal, dressed in his or her morning clothes and walking around looking like undertakers. The other reason was that I really felt that some time in my life I would like to be a general manager and one absolutely had to have a background in food and beverage so that one could talk intelligently to the chef and food and beverage staff. Apart from that,

I liked to eat and drink well.

My accent was also a disadvantage. It identified me as a public school boy and so-called upper class Englishman and that didn't go down too well with the chefs in the kitchen. They either thought you were some idiot, a sort of black sheep of the family (which was not too far from the truth) or worse still, a plant from management to spy on them to see whether they were running their kitchen properly. However, after reading the hotel and catering ads and keeping an eye on the local papers, I finally landed a job as a commie chef in a small restaurant. A commie is an assistant who helps in any department in the kitchen when he is needed which, in some cases, is great because you get to learn all aspects of the kitchen from sauces to roasts or soup to nuts.

The restaurant was called the Tudor Room and was in Bromley, a small town in Kent, not far from where I lived with my parents. The restaurant was well located on the main street, an attractive Tudor looking building with the typical white stucco walls, black wood beams and bay windows made of bottle glass, which looked like a Charles Dickens Curio Shop. Inside it was very tastefully decorated and seated around 80 people. The dining room staff was all female waitresses, which apparently put it in a very mediocre class as far as service. Not politically correct in today's world, but that's how the public of that time perceived it. The kitchens were quite large and had their own bakeshop where they made all their own desserts, bread and rolls. The chef was an absolute maniac. Later I was to find out that most of them were, but he worked very hard, long hours and drank consistently. The owner of the restaurant was a Jewish man who taught me my first lessons in food control. In the bake house, for instance, there was a large, four-gallon container where all the papers that the butter came wrapped in were placed and packed down with a weight on top. After a couple of weeks of compression, the container was put on a warm stove to melt all the butter left on the papers. Unbelievably, this method rescued a lot of butter. It was then used to grease pans for baking. The same thing applied to any cans of jams or marmalades that were opened. They were washed with hot water and rinsed into a large pot, which was then reduced to make glaze for the fruit tarts. He wasted absolutely nothing. I worked very hard and very long hours, getting in around 6 a.m. in the morning and leaving around 10 p.m. at night with a couple of hours off in the afternoon.

The chef, although an alcoholic, was an interesting character. Sometime in the past he had been saucier at Brown's Hotel in London, but the booze had go the better of him and he had slowly deteriorated ending up as the chef in this restaurant. Nevertheless he was a very talented man and started to teach me the basic sauces and stocks. It gave him pride to teaching someone. After he allowed me to make a sauce, if there was the slightest thing wrong with it, he would yell and scream and, if I was lucky, throw it into the dishwasher sink. Otherwise he might throw it clear across the kitchen aiming at my head. One day I was making a very simple demi-glaze when, because of the pressure of working in a kitchen, I forgot it and left it on the stove, burning not only the sauce, but also the pot, which was a good copper utensil. I couldn't believe that I had done this and knew that if the chef saw it he would go absolutely crazy. So, I decided to simply take the pot, put it in my locker upstairs and start again, which I did. Later, when I left to go home at 10 p.m., I carefully put the pot into a bag, took it home with me and, would you believe, buried it in the woods nearby the house so the chef could never find out that I ruined one of his sauces and the pot. That is how intimidated everyone was of chefs. After about six months of working with this maniac 7 days a week, I had really learned quite a bit. I had been allowed some time in the bake house where there was a very talented Dutchman who taught me how to make great puff pastries and sensational desserts. I then learned that a small but very exclusive hotel in Kensington on the outskirts of London was looking for an assistant saucier. I decided to apply for the position. The chef was a well-known man around London by the name of Trompetto. After interviewing me, and me having sold him on the fact that I was older than I was and that I really wanted to learn the art of cooking, he said that if I would care to work for one week without a salary, he would observe me and decide if he would hire me. I agreed and at the end of the week I was taken on.

Entering the kitchen of my first real hotel was quite an experience. A super heated world of stainless steel, a mass of raw and cooked food, raucous shouting in French and Italian, a wonderful atmosphere of frenzied industry, a Dante-esque microcosm filled with denizens clad in white high hats – my new world.

The Grand Hotel had a sensational, if small dining room seating about 60 people. The kitchen staff was small consisting of about 9 cooks, so apart from having the official title of Assistant Chef Saucier, I also had the opportunity to work in other departments, particularly if someone was sick or replacements were needed on someone's day off. I also got my first introduction to the hierarchy in the kitchen. The chef was absolute King to the point that the general manager of the hotel would never come into the kitchen. He would always ask the chef to go to his office. The cooks were a bunch of deviants, their main interest being drinking and porno pictures. The waiters were all Italian, absolute scum as far as the chef was concerned. The Maitre d' in this particular hotel was an old queen. The pot washers, yardmen and maids were all Irish immigrants and everyone fought like rattlesnakes.

The Maitre d' needed some pastries for an afternoon tea but he dared not cross the kitchen to pick them up himself so asked the chef to pass them to him. The chef, reading his request, simply ignored the waiter letting him know that he was busy having his lunch. The waiter then started to get a little excited changing from English to Italian. He finally called the chef something quite unflattering in Italian. At this point the chef stood up, picked up the silver dish and threw it with all his force across the kitchen at the waiter catching the poor man in the side of the head and literally felling him in the middle of the kitchen.

I got along well with the chef, probably because I was very young, worked hard and learned a lot in the process. The real unforgettable moment in my life at the Grand happened after working in the kitchen for about a week or so. One of the vegetable men stuck his head in the door and yelled, "They're at it again!" At which everyone rushed out of the kitchen like bats out of hell. I was so startled that I didn't really see where everyone went. They all returned 15 minutes later laughing uproariously and commenting on the perk that one gets when you are in management. I was intrigued but not stupid enough to ask what was going on. However, a week went by and the same thing happened again. Someone snapped their head in the kitchen door and yell, "They're at it again." This time I was near the door, so I followed closely on the heels of the roast cook as we raced through the back corridors and up two flights of stairs to a small room with a toilet bowl and above the toilet was a small window, approximately 12 by 8 inches. The room could barely hold two people. The window overlooked the courtyard. Somehow or another, the chef and about 12 other assorted people had beaten me to it. At least six people were standing on the toilet bowl, including the chef who must have weighed at least 250 pounds. At this point I couldn't see what they were all yelling about. But, they were encouraging someone by yelling and screaming, "Go at it!" I couldn't see a damn thing but I did find out that one could see the manager's office across a small light well where he could be seen as it was described as shagging his secretary, who was evidently quite an athletic and enthusiastic employee. It was a pity but I missed the whole show and I decided the next time I would go for a better seat. From then on when anyone yelled in the kitchen, I was ready to go. Sure enough about a week later (obviously he was quite regular in this activity) the signal came. I was up the two flights of stairs and the first one at the window brushing aside some waiter with an 18-inch French cooking knife who tried to get the better seat. Sure enough, there they were in all their glory. He was immaculately dressed in his morning suit, his dove gray waistcoat, striped tie and even a boutonniere in his lapel, but no pants, somewhat bizarre. He sort of looked like a penguin that had been shaved from the knees down. On the other hand, and I mean that literally, was this very attractive brunette and I might add, a true brunette, bent over the top of a very nice tooled leather desk, her face buried in the paperwork. Maybe she was trying to work at the same time. At least I gave her the benefit of the doubt. The manager attacked her from behind with the fervor of a pneumatic drill; it was a tantalizing sight. "So that's what the front of the house is like," I thought. I decided there and then that the front of the house must obviously be my future goal.

With all the timetables and pressures in the kitchen you could never get a little behind in your work, so to speak. Just when I was deliberating my future, the chef arrived, all 250 pounds of him, pushing everyone out of his way. He pulled himself up onto the toilet seat beside me to get a better view of the show at which time the whole bowl collapsed tumbling everyone onto the floor, leaving me grabbing onto the end of the chain, flushing it as I fell and filling everyone's shoes with water. I must say it was a fitting end to a fitting end. We all returned laughing to the kitchen and as I was working it was amusing to see that the butcher was stuffing the chickens with a great deal more enthusiasm. Everyone was animated and lots of talk went on for the next couple of hours.

Seeing that I was working very hard and that I was enthusiastic about my work, my father decided that I was obviously bent on learning the hotel business and decided that I should do it properly by attending a hotel school. He announced that he had inquired and got all the necessary papers from Westminster, which was the best hotel school in England at the time. He informed me that I would need a letter from my present employer, preferably the Managing Director, stating that I had worked in the hotel for a period of time, long enough at least for someone to have observed me and determine that I had the talent necessary to enter this very exclusive profession. My father asked if I thought I could get a good reference from the hotel. After giving it some careful thought, I said that I was sure that the Executive Office would bend over backwards to help me in furthering my education.

The next day after lunch I visited the executive offices for the first time. I must say his office was elegant. This was where the Managing Director, Mr. Sissons orchestrated the day-to-day goings-on. It was almost extravagant with paneling, oil paintings, fresh flowers, marble lamps, oriental rugs and a beautiful silver tea service from which they were just about to enjoy afternoon tea. The secretary, Ms. Harding, was as pretty close up as she was from atop the toilet seat, but she was a real snob and very priggish. As I entered the office I was greeted with a simple, "What do you want?" I explained whom I was which made zero impression on her. I eagerly explained that I was the one who created all those incredible sauces in the dining room, putting on as much charm as I could muster, then explaining that I needed a reference to attend hotel school so that I could further my career. She replied that Mr. Sissons never, under any circumstances, spoke directly with an employee. She told me that I should speak to my supervisor who would write a memo to Mr. Sissons who would, if he had time, consider the matter. However, since I was only a minor employee, it was highly unlikely he would write any letter of recommendation. He had certainly never done so in the past. Ms. Harding then dismissed me by studying my shoes, which made me feel I had stepped in something that the cat had brought in.

It was for me a real dilemma. I thought about my future and how important this reference was going to be and decided to approach the matter from a different angle. "Ms. Harding," I announced, "this letter, this reference is most important to me. From what I have observed you have a rather special relationship with the director and I am sure that if you extended yourself you could persuade him to give my reference some serious thought."

"What do you mean special relationship," she asked, still very snippy but a little caution entering her voice,"and what do you mean, from what you have observed?"

"Well," I said, pouring on all of my charm again, "there is a certain window across from the director's office where I have observed with a few close friends, the director shall we say, giving you a hard time." Seeing that I was making an impression, I decided to continue. "My camera," I said, "is not very sophisticated and the pictures though identifiable are not terribly good, but certainly would add an artistic bent to the employees bulletin board." I continued, "You know how it is, you have to use all your skills to get on in this world." Well, talk about a reaction. Either I was going to have to put something in her mouth to stop her from swallowing her tongue or find an instant cure for hyperventilation. She came around the desk like a whirlwind propelling me to the door and calling me all sorts of indelicate names. Once out of the earshot of the director's office she threatened to call the house detective and have me arrested. I suggested that we would be better perhaps discussing the problem with Mr. Sissons. Was she pissed! "Listen," I said, "let's not get excited, all I came up here for was a reference letter and you were the one who was uncooperative. I just decided that it was necessary to find a subject that we could have as a mutual starting point so that at least we could have some common social intercourse. Sorry, wrong word, I meant discourse. So, why don't you take hold of yourself and meet me at the Green Man, a pub down the street, at 6 p.m. after work and we will see if we can draft a letter setting out my excellent credentials." At this point I left her standing in the corridor of the executive office. Feeling that I had made my point and since it was almost five o'clock I went across to the library and sat in the quiet composing my reference letter. The

Green Man was a typical English pub, a place where office workers met after five for a couple of pints before going home. There was the proverbial dartboard and, I might add, a very attractive barmaid. I sat at a small table in the corner with my pint of Bass ale hoping that Ms. Harding would show up. Sure enough, she arrived even a few minutes early. She was still very hostile and wouldn't join me in a drink so I simply gave her my drafter letter. I suggested that she type it and have it signed as soon as possible by Mr. Sissons. She left in a huff – most ungracious for a Managing Director's secretary.

I never did get to meet the Managing Director, but a call came to the kitchen the next morning. It was Ms. Harding suggesting that we meet at the front door at lunchtime, which I readily agreed. I was there waiting with anticipation when she arrived, giving me the letter like a good sport. I opened it and read it; it was just as I had written it. I was not sure if it was the Managing Director's signature, but what the hell - it looked good. I slipped it into my pocket. She said with flushed cheeks, "You must not return to the hotel and, what about the photos?" I almost said, "What photos" and I was tempted to suggest that she come by my apartment that evening to see if we could reenact some of the scenes. Maybe that was pushing it a bit too far, especially since I didn't have any photos. I simply said, "Well, I will have to send them to you in a plain wrapper since they were really too lewd to carry around in public" I left her with a farewell suggestion to keep her end up and her nose to the grindstone. She really was a pill. As a matter of interest, some time later I met the chef at a local pub and he asked me why I left so suddenly. He also told me that, for some unknown reason, they had reglazed the window with frosted glass in the bathroom spoiling the weekly entertainment. I was of course delighted since it meant the signature on the letter was probably genuine. It also meant they were at it again – Rule Britannia. My father was delighted with my reference letter, suggesting that I must have made quite an impression on someone.

Westminster College was also impressed with my reference since I started on my City & Guilds courses the next month

CHAPTER FOUR

Hotel School And Trade Experience

H otel school was the best thing that ever happened to me. Sixty percent of the learning process was practical. Great chefs, mostly retired from some of the best hotels in London and other European cities, taught how to prepare and create everything from delicate sauces to exotic desserts. Maitre d's with impeccable backgrounds taught how to correctly wait on tables, using the various methods of English, French and Russian service. The school had its own restaurant that was open to the public so that one had real experience waiting on customers.

Experts demonstrated how to pull sugar, which was a very delicate art and used a great deal in those days. It was the art of pulling sugar into beautiful designs of flowers and baskets and decorations for the tops of cakes. Butchers showed how to break down a side of beef or a whole sheep.

Every two months or so you had a practical test. The tests were actually preparing an extensive five or six course dinner from a variety of raw products. You would have a station, which consisted of a table, an oven and stove and all the necessary utensils. Piled on top of the table would be a variety of raw pieces of meat, spices, vegetables, flour, butter, and sugar, all the things needed to make the meal. You could even have a live chicken or a live lobster tied to the leg of the table, which you then had to kill and prepare for cooking. You were then given a menu and a certain amount of time to prepare the meal and serve it. You were judged by two or three chefs who would decide how well you had done. They would taste everything and see whether you used the correct cuts of meat, the proper ingredients, the correct seasoning and, if you made say a crème caramel, if the texture was right.

On one occasion, a young lady in our class who was studying to be a catering supervisor in a hospital was given a huge three-pound lobster. She was absolutely terrified of it. She was boiling the water in which to cook the lobster, and was testing it frequently to see if it was hot enough. One of the chefs boomed out, "Young lady, are you going to give that lobster a bath, or are you going to cook it?" This might not seem to be very dramatic, but when one of these master chefs spoke, it was enough to put the fear of God into you. It completely destroyed this young lady's confidence.

I was very good and whether it was a matter of making a very complex sauce or executing French or Russian service in the restaurant for a table full of experts, nothing seemed to phase me. It was very simple once I was shown something. I enjoyed not only repeating what I was shown, but also doing it with a flair. I found it much easier to be instructed this way rather than swatting over books. Of course management and accounting methods and techniques were also taught, but I was really attracted to the kitchen. It seemed to be an exciting mixture of nationalities, incredible smells and tastes, and

*At hotel school Tremain learns how to carve center pieces
for banquets out of tallow, or fat, or ice.*

a kitchen was always busy trying to meet a deadline, whether it is for breakfast, lunch, dinner or a banquet. There was always a tense excitement. I quickly became a first class student and would in fact finally pass out of Westminster with honors.

I was living back at my grandmothers in North London near Hampstead and traveling by tube into the City of London to school each day. During my lunch hours and after school, I spent time wandering around London, particularly visiting some of the great pubs. Here I would consistently find the waiters and kitchen staff passing their time between shifts. Consequently, I was invited to visit some of the great hotel and restaurant kitchens of London.

The pubs were also very famous and each had its own character and clientele. For instance, one pub on Bond Street, the Capatz, catered to the bowler hat crowd who were importers of everything from the teas of India to furs of Northern Canada. One tradition that this pub had was to leave your bowler hat at the door on a special rack. It was almost a tourist attraction to come in and see rows of bowler hats. The pubs on Fleet Street were the hangouts of all the journalists and you could always find the latest gossip and news. Other pubs I like just because of their names, such as The Mucky, The Keys, Number 7, and there was a place called the Tiger Tavern, which is opposite the Tower of London. You could arrive via river steamer at tower pier and enter the pub through a secret passage. There was also a pub, which I could never remember the name of but that it had a boxing ring upstairs. Of course, there was Dirty Dicks, which was known, as the filthiest bar in London, but actually most of it is fake décor and done purely for effect. All this was very cheap entertainment because you could sit and pass away the hours sipping on a pint of beer and simply socialize.

It was because of my pub-crawling that I was also invited to become an apprentice member of the International Society of Chefs de Cuisine. This was a loosely knit group of chefs who used to get together to try to further their cause. Of course in those days there were no unions. Working conditions were very difficult and if nothing else, everyone got together just to bitch about all these problems.

I passed my City and Guilds 101, the basic food and beverage exam and stayed another year but then decided not to go on for more exotic courses. I was desperate to get live experience and find a job.

CHAPTER FIVE

A Royal Treat

On one or two occasions while attending one of the meetings in a local pub I sat next to a man who I guessed was in his mid-70's. He had taken a liking to me, I think because of my enthusiasm in discussing the intricacies of dishes and food with him. He introduced himself as Gabriel Tschumi, the Royal Chef. I encouraged him to talk and found him absolutely fascinating. He told me that he came to England in 1898 as a young apprentice and worked at Buckingham Palace. He had an incredible memory and talked about a garden party he organized for Queen Victoria held on the grounds of Buckingham Palace in July, 1900. He also organized the Coronation Banquet that never happened, for King Edward VII. He told me they had prepared the total banquet, which was an incredible extravaganza with 14 courses that were approved by King Edward and Queen Alexandra. He was the chef on a boat with King George V called the Maid of Orleans, which crossed from Dover to Calais in 1916. He told me he was on very personal terms with Queen Mary. I simply let him talk and just wished I had a tape

35

recorder to capture the total story from him. One day he told me that he was about to prepare probably the last birthday party that he would prepare and that Queen Mary would probably be alive to see. Much to my surprise, and I think it was because of my young age, he suggested that I might like to come over to the Marlborough House and work for two or three days and assist in preparing the birthday party and then be there for the serving of it on the 26th of May, 1952, which was Queen Mary's birthday. Well, as you can imagine, I jumped at the opportunity and on May 21st arrived at Marlborough House.

The kitchens were large, typical I suppose of an old house or castle, but it had high airy windows, which looked out, over the driveway. I was surprised that things like the refrigerators and wine cellars were quite up to date. The stoves were vast gas ranges and the place was spotlessly clean. I was fascinated and arrived at 6:30 a.m. to find Tschumi already in his office. The first order of the day was to prepare Queen Mary's breakfast tray, which was sent up to her in her sitting room at 9 a.m. on the dot every day. I discovered she did not believe in large breakfasts and simply had coffee, toast, butter, marmalade and fresh fruit and of course everything was of the highest quality. Interestingly enough, she approved all the menus and when the breakfast tray went up in the morning, the menus for the next two days, both lunch and dinner, were sent up with it. She reviewed them, made certain pencil suggestions on them and sent them back to the chef. After breakfast, the kitchen got down to preparing lunch for the Queen and her staff. Although the staff had simpler meals than those of the Queen, they certainly ate very well. There seemed to be a large number of personnel around and I was told that there were probably 70 or 80 people looking after the Queen in Marlborough House. I did not get to meet many of them and I understand it was about half of what she used to have in earlier days.

It turns out that the birthday tea was not an elaborate affair, but the making of the cakes was. I say cakes, in the plural, because there were five cakes made so that she could share them with various groups of people.

The first was simply a very light sponge cake, beautifully decorated. Served with the cake were sandwiches and biscuits. On the 26th of May, which was her birthday, shortly before midday, she was driven in her green Daimler to Buckingham Palace where she had lunch with other members of the royal family and then returned to Marlborough House later in the afternoon for her tea. For this particular occasion, the cake had a chocolate icing in four layers and then filled with fresh cream and simply the words on top, "Hearty Congratulations." It sounds simple, but it was a most beautifully decorated cake and Tschumi did the decorations himself. Around 4 the cake was put onto a tea wagon and wheeled in by a footman to Queen Mary where she shared this particular cake with her ladies in waiting and from what I gather, some close friends. One cake she took over to Buckingham Palace to share with her great grandchildren, Prince Charles and Princess Ann. Obviously, she kept a busy schedule.

One thing that was interesting was the preparation of the tea. I particularly remember this and wrote it down. It was served in an antique silver tea service, which had belonged to Queen Victoria. Following the cakes would come another trolley on which a kettle was placed on a spirit burner. She would make the tea herself. The ceremony included measuring the India Tea from a Jade Chinese tea caddy that she kept especially in the cabinet of her sitting room. Once she had made the tea, it was allowed to brew for exactly three minutes. Then, the footman was given the signal to pour. It was a ceremony that even through the cracks of the door was impressive.

I kept in touch with Tschumi and he told me some months later, I think it was in September, that he had resigned his position at Marlborough House so that he could retire with his wife to his house in the country. It was an interesting experience for me, one that I shall never forget. As I look back on it, it was a privilege to be admitted into the inner sanctums of Marlborough House.

CHAPTER SIX

Soho, The Melting Pot Of London

Through a contact I made at one of the Society meetings, I discovered that I could get myself a job in the evenings, which suited me fine because I was really only going to school from 9 a.m to 4 p.m. so I had lots of time to spare. This would give me some good experience in working in a commercial establishment. As it turned out, the job that was being offered was in a restaurant called the Café Bleu in Soho. In those days, Soho was a very exciting place in London. A cross section of everything and everyone – theater people, dignitaries, prostitutes, strippers. It was the film center of Great Britain and had ethnic food shops all over the place. They had every conceivable type of restaurant. It was really the melting pot of England's best and most informed by their own admission.

The Café Bleu was a typical French bistro with 40 seats and a small bar. It was quite elegant with white tablecloths, great silver and lots of mirrors. Both the restaurant and the bar were situated at the back and divided by white draperies from the front of the restaurant where there was a counter seating from 10 to 12 people. The counter was very elegantly set up with silver and nice linen place mats. You could get anything from the menu, but the local favorite was a sensational sandwich carved to order off huge smoked hams and turkeys which were displayed on those old fashioned marble stands with a huge spike in the middle. The chef would carve the ham or the breast of turkey right in front of you onto some special bread. You could also have an omelet made right there in front of you. It was quite expensive and very busy. My job was to be the counter chef and I worked from 7 in the evening until midnight. I found my clientele to be affluent and extremely varied. It could range from lawyers and bankers who were taking a meal at the end of the workday and then going back to the office, to couples going to the theater, to showgirls from the Windmill Theater having a late night dinner, to one or two very expensive call girls with beaucoup money and lots of style.

The evenings were never dull. I was very conservative and somewhat of a curiosity to most of the customers since they had never met a chef with a British public school accent. I was also 6ft 4" without my chefs hat and as thin as a string bean. I was certainly an oddity to be working in Soho. The showgirls in particular always loved to tease me and one night during intermission at the Windmill, six showgirls turned up to sit at the counter. They were all well over 6 feet, which was a requirement to be a dancer. They were British, as most of the showgirls were, even at the Lido in Paris. They all wore what looked like to me expensive fur coats. It was the month of November and was quite cold and damp at night, so it was not unusual to see them all come in their fur coats. They proceeded to give me their orders, which included various sandwiches and a couple of omelets. At one point I turned around to take care of the omelets. When I turned back, much to my surprise, the six girls were all sitting there naked under their fur coats with their very ample breasts resting on the counter. No one else in the restaurant could see this because they sat with their elbows on the counter and held their coats so that only I would notice the condition they were in. I turned as red as a beetroot which brought giggles galore from the girls. It was obviously a well-planned joke on me. One of my regular customers who came in at least two or three times a week was an extremely beautiful woman that I guessed to be around 24 or 25, dressed in the most expensive and exquisite fashions of the day. She also wore the most unbelievable jewelry that I had ever seen, including at least an 8-carat ring. Her car, a black Jaguar, was driven by a young Asian chauffeur dressed in high boots and cap, the typical chauffeur uniform and he would wait for her outside. I was told by one of the assistant managers that she was probably one of the most expensive call girls in London and among her client list were members of Parliament and British aristocrats. It turns out that her name was Pamela. She fascinated me and we became good friends. She was insistent on not being disturbed, but she liked me and enjoyed having someone to talk to while she was having dinner and the times she came in were not very busy for me. She never explained what she did for a living, not that I felt she had to, and of course I never asked. She would discuss world affairs, the political kind, and theater. She was obviously a very well educated woman. I suppose with the type of people that she mixed, she had to pick up a lot of what they were about. My father called me one day and told me that to celebrate my grandmother's 93rd birthday the family was going to go to the famous Trocadero restaurant and then on to a show to see Dial M for Murder. If I could get a night off, they would like me to join and if I would like to bring somebody that would be just fine. With my work schedule I didn't really know anyone I could take to the theater. But as it happened, the night before we were to go to the theater, who came in but Pamela. As normal we chatted about the days headlines in the newspaper and I told her about the occasion and explained to her that I was going with my family to the Trocadero and then on to the theater to see Dial M for Murder and if she would like to, I would love her to join us. She was obviously very amused. She said that I was a very unusual and charming young man and, yes, she would love to join me, but asked if I was sure that I knew what I was doing. I didn't really think about what she was asking me. I told her I just thought she was an extremely beautiful woman and I was very surprised and delighted that she accepted. She explained that she would pick me up in front of the Hyde Park Hotel the next evening at quarter 'til seven. I could not believe my luck!

Sure enough, the next night promptly at quarter 'til seven up rolls Pamela in her black Jaguar, complete with driver. We then drove to the Trocadero restaurant where my family, my grandmother, stepmother, father, brother and his wife, were all waiting outside. They were more than a little surprised to see me step out of a chauffeur driven car and then I think a little aghast when they saw Pamela. She had on an elegant black Chanel suit, very expensive pearls with a large diamond clasp and a Russian Sable coat. She was so impeccably dressed she couldn't possibly have looked like her profession, but she obviously didn't look like a normal 24 year-old either. She had I think deliberately dressed to look conservative and I must admit I was no slouch either. I was earning good money and spending a lot of it on clothes. I thought we made quite a pair, but I could see everyone was shocked. My father was known in some of the gentlemen's clubs around town, but he was not that well known at places like the Trocadero. However, Pamela obviously was. We were all made a big fuss of and seated at the best table in the restaurant. Conversation was a little strained but Pamela held her own. She discussed everything from politics to the national budget and all through dinner she made a big fuss of me, making sure I had enough wine. At one point, she even slipped me a five-pound note to give to the Maitre d'. She could see that my father obviously wasn't going to give him that much money and she had to come back. The family was totally nonplussed at the whole show. At one time, my grandmother, in her very Victorian British manner, asked looking directly at me, "Pray, how did you two meet?" which, before I choked, Pamela promptly answered that we had met over drinks at Lord Thompson's flat in Mayfair. He was a well-known newspaper tycoon and I wouldn't have known him if he had sat in front of me at the restaurant counter. I smiled rather sickly and this brought everyone to his or her feet, after what had been a wonderful dinner. We continued the evening by going to see the play. I think my father was amused by the whole incident, suggesting to me that I was moving in rather fast circles but, in fact, he enjoyed talking to Pamela much to the chagrin of my stepmother. My grandmother, at one point during the evening, pulled me aside and said it was time that I started to save money and settle down. She then proceeded to not speak to me for at least a month.

Pamela and I became very good friends. She appeared to enjoy my friendship which I suspected was quite contrary too her other life. It was probably a pleasant change of pace. We did funny things, like going to the London zoo, taking the train to the beach at Brighton and she insisted on taking me to dinner in some small, very fashionable French restaurants that, despite my earning power, would have wiped me out overnight. On a couple of occasions, I stayed over at her magnificent Mayfair apartment. I told everyone at home that I missed the last tube home. It never became a business relationship, which I think was rather fortunate since I would have probably been bankrupt at an early age. Strangely enough she loved to cook a wonderful dinner, bringing out the candles and putting on the right music. It was as if she preferred the seducing for a change and I certainly didn't complain.

Hotel school was coming to an end. I had completed my education with honors including my extra curricular activities and I now found it necessary to get a serious job. So, like half the hotel profession in London, I went to visit Alfred Marks, an employment agency in Soho that specialized in placing you in a hotel or restaurant. Alfred Marks consisted of a large room with three or four people sitting behind desks and what appeared to be rolls of toilet paper. On the back of them were listed numerous jobs around London, other parts of England and the continent. It was always full of hotel people looking to further their position.

CHAPTER SEVEN

The Real World

There were a number of jobs being offered, none of which seemed terribly interesting until the elderly lady who was taking care of me said, "If you have been working in front of the public at the Café Bleu, then here is an interesting job for you. It's a Chef de Rang at the Dorchester Hotel on Park Lane." The Chef de Rang is the showman who cooks at your table on a garadon, a portable spirit burner, combining the skills of a chef and that of a captain waiter. The lady said, "You are a bit young but why don't you at least go down and interview for the job?"

The Dorchester was one of London's great hotels. The McAlpine family then owned it, evidently with immense holdings in everything except the Bank of England. I found the employment office and was immediately ushered up to be interviewed by one of the assistant Maitre d's. I lied a little about my age. In fact I looked much older than I really was, and that I had worked in several restaurants in London. Interestingly in those days, they didn't really check out your references.

What they did was put you to the test. He promptly gave me a couple of mushrooms and a knife and asked me to turn a mushroom. This was not a complicated operation. It's simply accomplished by taking the mushroom in one hand and with the tip of the knife fluting the mushroom all around to look like a flower. It was very decorative and used quite frequently. He then asked me to make a Hollandaise sauce and then prepare a sole Colbert, which takes a little skill in the filleting of a large whole sole. This I did with a great deal of skill. He was duly impressed and I was told to report for work that evening at 4 p.m. in the main dining room.

It was to my uninitiated eyes, a very grand dining room. Since I was the last one hired, I was delegated to what was considered the worst station in the restaurant farthest away from the kitchen, which meant a lot of walking. My associate was an old waiter who constantly had a runny nose and a stained apron. However, as slow as he was, he was greatly skilled and allowed me to take my time in the preparation of dishes since we really didn't have all that many people to wait on anyway. He constantly wanted to add a little of this and a little of that to the dishes to impress the customer. He knew all the tricks of the trade. For instance, when I was sautéing something in a pan over the fire, he would put fingers surreptitiously in a glass of water and flamboyantly gesture at the pan, grabbing the attention of the guest. The drops of water would drop into the pan, igniting the pan with flames, making him look like some magician. In fact, we ended up a pretty good team.

The dining room was staffed with captains and waiters who were racing addicts. At every opportunity they would be leaving the dining room to place bets on the horses or the dogs. In having lost most of their money at the tracks and being perpetually hungry, they surreptitiously filched the food off the dishes that were brought into the dining room from the kitchen. From this, they had developed an incredible ability to eat something in the dining room in front of the customer without moving their mouths.

My captain, Mr. Sarti was one of those who was always eating on the job. On one occasion when I was serving a magnificent cream soup to a party of six, Mr. Sarti slipped an olive into his mouth to eat it non-mesticato, in other words, without moving his mouth. Suddenly, just as I was placing the final soup dish in front of the host, he coughed and the pit from the olive shot out of his mouth between a missing tooth and went directly into the soup plate of the woman sitting at the head of the table. I was the only one who saw it besides the captain and I could see he was mortified. I barely controlled myself from not roaring with laughter. He immediately made the pretense of wiping the edge of the soup plate with a napkin and at the same time trying to remove the plate from in front of the lady. However, she firmly took hold of the plate thinking he was attempting to clear the table and began to sip her soup. My captain and I looked at each other – sensing a catastrophe. We were both going to lose our jobs and cause an unholy commotion in the dining room. My warped sense of humor tempted me to let her finish and see what happened, but finally my better judgment won out and I decided to save the day. I wheeled my garidon to her side and waited for her to put down her spoon for a second. Much to her surprise I whipped the plate from underneath her and said that I would be delighted to serve her a touch more. Before she could refuse, I scooped out the olive pit, added a touch more soup and replaced the dish in front of her in a matter of seconds. The day was saved, but I might add, it never stopped Mr. Sarti from eating during the service of a meal.

CHAPTER EIGHT

The King And I

One day the Maitre d' came to our station and told Mr. Sarti and I that a Royal from Denmark was coming to dinner with a guest and had requested to be seated in our station. He added that he was astonished as we were. Seeing that Sarti had no explanation he said, "Well, don't ask me, but he insists on your station and he obviously has a good reason. He will have two plain-clothes security guards at another table and no one else will sit near them. They are the only people you will have on your station and they will arrive at approximately 8:30 p.m." Mr. Sarti and I waited, amused and in obvious anticipation. Sarti thought either someone remembered him from the old days or it was a crazy mistake. Promptly at 8:30 two security men arrived surveying the dining room as they walked in. There was quite a commotion as the Royal couple arrived, and who was on his arm, "the most beautiful woman in the world" – Pamela. Mr. Sarti pulled her chair out and she sat with the faintest smile nodding to me. I, of course, kept a stiff upper lip. Sarti and I performed like the perfect team we were and were rewarded with

47

an extremely large tip; probably the largest Mr.Sarti had ever seen. The Maitre'd kept hovering around and asking me why the Royal had asked for our station, as indeed did Mr. Sarti. I could hardly tell them that it was because I went to bed with the gentleman's mistress because they would have laughed me out of the hotel and even I thought it was a little unbelievable.

For the next few months Pamela would come in with very important people who not only made our station the most sought after in the dining room, but also made Mr. Sarti and I the best-paid team in the hotel. I continued to see Pamela on the odd occasion still thinking the whole affair was quite bizarre. But who was I to interfere with the good things in life.

I soon found out that there were all sorts of deals going on in the hotel amongst the employees. One was the illicit use of one of the most opulent suites in the hotel called the Oliver Messell Suite. When it was not rented for some outrageous price, some of the captains and waiters would bribe the front desk staff with a great meal to give them a key and use it for their own little card games and frequently spent the night there. It should also be noted that most of the waiters in London in those days slept in the restaurant since they really earned no salary at all, surviving only on tips. Very few of them had anywhere to sleep anyway since they were newly arrived immigrants from Italy and other European countries. They would, after the restaurant closed, slip back into the dining room and stretch out on a banquette covering themselves with a side of the table and letting the tablecloth fall over the top of them. This was done so that if anyone came into the dining room, they would not see the waiter asleep, just the tablecloths on the tables covering part of the banquettes. The waiter would then be ready, waiting to serve breakfast at the crack of dawn. Most of the waiters worked at least 14 hours a day in the dining room with a split shift having time off between meals.

CHAPTER NINE

A Count of No Account

Even though most of the employees who were working around London in those days were as perverse as they were diverse, that's what makes hotel life at least interesting.

There were con men, jailbirds who were hiding out, husbands who were hiding from ex-wives and parole jumpers who were on the lamb. But, one man in particular, a dishwasher, was fascinating.

He was an Italian by the name of Amelio and seemed to have the airs and manners of an elegant background. You could tell that just by looking at him. He was quiet and never really spoke to anyone. He simply did his job. And he did it impeccably.

I started to gain his confidence and found out that he was a former count, from a noble Italian family, who had become an alcoholic and skidded down the familiar path and ended up washing dishes in the Dorchester Hotel. He was a charming man and soon started telling me stories of the "Bellavita."

One day, when reading the week's banquet list, I noticed an upcoming important Italian charity dinner. Listed on the back of the menu were the sponsors, a lot of which were Italian aristocrats. I showed Amelio the invitation and the menu. It almost brought tears to his eyes. He shook his head knowingly as he recognized some of the names.

A little later, several of us in the kitchen and a couple of the banquet captains were having a beer in the local pub and decided it would be fun to sort of do a Cinderella thing and send this wonderful Italian count, who was now of no account, to this very important social event.

That very evening I arranged to borrow a tuxedo from one of the captains who was off that night, and had the dishwashing count's name included on the guest list by a friend of mine who worked in the banquet office. We also, unbeknown to anyone, simply added an extra seat and a place setting at the table. I told Amelio that it was all arranged and that he was listed on the guest list as Count Amelio de Gorgoza Pasini. How about that for a name?

The Maitre d' and waiters thought it a fabulous joke that their dishwasher would be injected in the aristocracy that filled the ballroom of the Dorchester. I must say we were all very impressed with Amelio's appearance that night. He looked splendid in the tuxedo. His shoes were polished to the point that you could see your face in them and his black hair was glossy with Brylcream, a famous English hair dressing in those days, and parted in the middle. For the occasion he had pinned a few of his old medals on his chest. He looked the part as if he was from central casting. The Maitre d's and waiters made a big fuss of him as he carried on magnificently at his table. We all watched him from the kitchen door. His past wore well. It had never left him. Once a count always a count.

Wine brings on a glow and, with Italians, the need to express themselves. As the evening proceeded someone from each table would rise, glass in hand making toasts and counter toasts. At one point the count stood up and everyone who was in on the charade froze.

"My God, he is going to make a speech," I exclaimed to everyone in the kitchen and they all rushed to the door. Instead, he simply turned around and walked out of the ballroom having the graciousness and common sense to know when he had had enough.

I told him about the fright he had given us. He smiled and said, "Caro, I thank you and the others for what you did for me. My hands may be in dishwater, but my head is now in the clouds."

I just had to give this gentleman a big hug.

CHAPTER TEN

The Buyer

Sometimes I would work a breakfast banquet arriving around 4:30 or 5 in the morning and on these occasions I would always run into a gentleman in an impeccable long white coat and straw hat. He would be sipping a cup of tea in the employee dining room. I often wondered who he was to be dressed like that so early in the morning. It turns out his name was John Gillespie. He was the meat and produce buyer for the hotel. His job took him to the markets at unearthly hours, in the early part of the morning when the markets were at their busiest. I asked him if one day I may accompany him to see them in action. He said, "Sure, if you want to be around at 2 a.m. in the morning, I would be more than happy to take you."

So a week later when I finished work in the dining room at about 1 a.m., I waited around and John picked me up and off we went to buy meat at Smithfield Market. He seemed very pleased that someone was interested in, what he explained, was one of the most important jobs of the hotel. As a matter of fact, he was correct because it didn't matter how great the chef was, if he didn't have first class meat and produce to work with, his efforts would be wasted. On the other hand, everything was properly stacked in the refrigerators and the storerooms before the kitchen really started to work, so everyone took his work for granted.

If someone told me that I'd be in a traffic jam at 3 a.m. I would have said that there were not that many drunks floating around London at that time to create one. Nevertheless, there it was. Smithfield Market was a mob scene. In and all around the market there were buyers from all over England vying for the "best cut." As I entered the market proper, I was immediately struck by three vivid colors – red, white and blue – British to say the least. The steel framework of the building was painted a bright blue. The thousands upon thousands of carcasses hanging on hooks were of the color of blood red, and the white was the hundreds of salesmen's long coats. They took great pride in their spotless white coats and starched collars. They wore their straw hats at a jaunty angle and during their animated bargaining continually told jokes and laughed uproariously.

The place was incredibly clean and the only hazardous moments during the buying was when the big porters, and they were big brawny fellows, would come charging through the alleyways with loads of carcasses totally oblivious to anyone that they might mow down with their huge sides of beef. I followed Mr. Gillespie as he inspected dozens of carcasses. After what appeared to be a lot of prodding and prying with his fingers, he stuck a skewer into one of them. Each skewer had an insignia, which indicated a Dorchester purchase. When he had finished buying what I thought was an enormous amount of lamb, beef, veal, sausages and sides of bacon, I asked him if he did this every week. "Every week?" he exclaimed, "This will all be gone by the end of dinner tonight, laddie. I will be here the same time tomorrow."

The only females that I saw during the entire buying trip were some nuns, which indeed surprised me. Mr. Gillespie told me that they were from various orphanages and they came every day to get what food they could for the orphans. The buyers evidently were very generous in contributing from their lots.

The last item he bought was several hundred pounds of fat, which the kitchen staff would render down for deep-frying. In those days every piece of meat was trimmed in the hotel butchers shop and carefully rendered down to use for frying fish in the big fish fryers. Today a hotel just buys the fat in bulk from a supplier.

"How does all this get in here?" I questioned. "They certainly can't get it in through that traffic jam outside." "Follow me, lad," he instructed. I followed Mr. Gillespie into a huge elevator probably 20 feet long and 10 feet wide, which descended into an enormous cavernous space. There was an entire railroad station underground through which the meat arrived from all over the world to feed one of the largest cities in the world. It was a rare experience to see this unusual nightlife. On returning to the hotel Mr. Gillespie always entered through the front door, not the employee's entrance. He would talk to the Maitre d's about the weeks business, tell the storerooms what to expect and then do his rounds of the kitchens.

I'd never seen a hotel waking up before. It was just 6 a.m. To me it was a dramatic experience to see this giant stirring out of its slumber. In the front of the hotel waiters were arriving, desk clerks were taking up their positions at the front desk; house porters were polishing furniture and floors. I walked through the double doors from the main dining room into the kitchen – my world for the last two or three years. It was a frenzied industry, a world of racket, which, reverberating amongst metal and earth-ware, was absolutely deafening. A world of white - the many chefs, all with white coats, aprons and hats, were bustling to and from the stoves to the refrigerators. In a few hours I had gone from a teaming, bustling market to the awakening of a "Grande Dame" to a Dante's inferno of a kitchen.

I also realized that a year had gone past very fast and that I had worked in the dining room, the banquet kitchens, the main kitchen and even for two weeks, while someone was on vacation, covered as an assistant Maitre d' in the main dining room. It was all a great experience, but I wasn't sure it was particularly getting me anywhere in the hotel business. I was starting to think more seriously about my future. I decided that if, in fact, my ambition was to be a General Manager then I had to make the crossover to the front of the house. So, I started once again to visit Alfred Marks and read the Catering Journal to see what jobs were available.

CHAPTER ELEVEN

The Front Of The House

Funny enough, as soon as I made the conscious decision to move to the front of the house, my British public school accent became very useful. In fact, everyone including the employment offices at Alfred Marks seemed to understand now that what I had been doing for the last couple of years was working around to get experience and that now I was ready to be serious about my future. I attended a couple of interviews for assistant managers, tending still to lean towards food and beverage and, I think, I was very good material.

I decided to accept the job as assistant manager at the Palace Hotel in Kensington. It was a small hotel by today's standards, 60 guest rooms, a few suites, a main dining room, a small grill with a very nice men's bar off of it and three very elegant banquet rooms, holding about 20 to 50 people. My responsibilities were to be the assistant manager in charge of all food and beverage operations. The only other assistant manager was a lady front office person in charge of the reception desk and reservations who had been with the hotel for 15 years.

I was for all intents and purposes the number two man. I served as the front of the house manager, working all hours of the day, sometimes from 7 in the morning until 9 at night, but I loved it. I was still only 19 but everyone thought I was 24, mainly because I told them I was, and I also looked as if I was 24.

The Director of the hotel, Kenneth Goodman, was a smooth looking London Jew in his 50's. He constantly smoked a cigar in a holder and looked like an Italian film director or a high-class gangster. He had worked his whole life in the hotel business. He spoke four or five languages and had worked in hotels all around the world. I liked him. He had a lot of style and we got along well together. He lived with his wife in the hotel, but also had a small house in Surrey where he used to spend weekends. After a few weeks he had so much confidence in me he asked me to move into the hotel on Thursday night and live in the hotel until Monday noon. I ate in the dining room, wore striped pants and a morning suit, a carnation in the lapel and commanded a great deal of respect amongst the employees, or at least I thought I did.

The hotel ran pretty smoothly. It was always busy. The dining room was full and had many regular repeat guests coming back time and time again. It was not done to fraternize with the guests however.

CHAPTER TWELVE

The Opera Singer

Patronize – yes; to fraternize – no. There was no law against it, but it simply wasn't done. However, there was a wonderful opera singer staying in the hotel for some weeks. She was performing at the Savoy in a Gilbert and Sullivan operetta. She was about 40 and quite beautiful in a crazy gypsy-like way and had huge breasts. She was, in fact, Hungarian. At around 10:30 or 11 each night she would arrive with a great flourish in the lobby, wearing a huge fur cape and long flowing gowns, demanding something to eat and drink. The last dinner orders were taken at 9:30 p.m., so the kitchen and room service were officially closed. However, I thought she was just sensational and would do anything for her. First of all, she was very pleasant besides being beautiful. Her skin was so creamy, it was delicious. So, I would go down to the kitchen and rustle something up for her. Then, she would insist that I share a glass of wine with her in the dining room, which I didn't mind in the least, it broke the routine. Especially when Goodman was away, it was sort of fun to talk to someone so eccentric.

She would wave her arms, sing loudly and attract everyone's attention. One night she called in advance and exclaimed, "Tonight I want to eat in my suite" and asked if I would care to come up and personally serve her as it was her birthday and wanted to celebrate. She then proceeded to order some fresh pâté, a complete cold duck, two bottles of champagne and a bottle of Chateau d'Yquem with some fresh poached peaches. "Enough for two," she said.

Some of the kitchen staff were still around so I rustled up the dinner, gave it to room service and, as requested, went up with them. I was very curious and wanted to see who the male leading impresario was going to be. I didn't realize that she had the finest suite in the hotel. I hadn't really inspected all of the suites because that was not my domain and I was duly impressed with the elegance and size of her suite.

As usual, she arrived with a magnificent flourish. She looked magnificent in her long black gown with rows of pearls. Room service had set up the table in the suite so I accompanied her inside. Upon walking into the room she let down her long black hair, which was normally piled, on top of her head. She insisted that I open the champagne and that I sit down and have dinner with her. I was surprised and asked if she was not expecting a guest. "NO, no, no" she sang at the top of her voice, "You my love, are my guest tonight." I was going to explain that this could get me fired but, to hell with it, it would be fun. We promptly got delightfully drunk together. She was very funny, breaking into song between mouthfuls of duck and champagne. Within an hour or so we were both quite drunk but very happy. She suddenly insisted that I run a bath, to fill it with scented bath foam and join her in the bath with the bottle of Chateau d'Yquem and the peaches.

At that time of night I thought it sounded pretty good, so I promptly ran the bath, which was incidentally one of those wonderful, old fashioned, huge bathtubs. I filled it with a wonderful scented bath gel, collected the ice bucket with the rest of the champagne and the bottle of Chateau d'Yquem, stepped into the bath and started to relax. All of a sudden the bathroom door burst open to an aria of Madama Butterfly and there stood the largest singing woman I have ever seen. She had more breast than the whole chorus line of the Windmill Theater. She was huge and immediately stepped into the bath holding a large silver bowl of freshly poached peaches, marinated in liquor and promptly sat down with a thump. I thought I would drown in the ensuing tidal wave of soapsuds. The water went over the top and completely flooded the bathroom.

She continued to keep singing and I was in a hysterical euphoria, laughing like an idiot. The bath had a wire rack that bridged the bath to hold the soap, nail file and back brushes. Something you don't see today. She tossed out the brushes flinging them across the room with a flourish and set up a buffet table on the wire rack. We then proceeded to eat the peaches and finish off the wine. Talk about a Roman orgy or perhaps a comic opera. A little later the opera singer proceeded to dance me into an enormous four-poster bed. It had to be to accommodate this singer and I was a willing actor. She commenced to entice me into bed, which was not very difficult in my state. But I was having a great deal of trouble making love to her because, not only was it difficult to get on top of her since it felt like I was trying to stay atop a floating rubber balloon, but extremely difficult to penetrate her, which for some reason or other made her laugh uproariously and start singing again. At this point I felt like I had an out of control wild bull in a rodeo cage. I was concerned I was going to fall off and kill myself since it seemed like a great distance to the floor. And, if she ever fell on top of me my hotel career would have come to an abrupt end. So much for satisfying your guests' every whim. I walked around in a daze for the rest of the weekend.

The rest of the year passed without incident. I learned a great deal about running a hotel from Mr. Goodman, from purchasing to serving elegant banquets to satisfying lords and opera singers. But I had itchy feet and decided maybe I should do some traveling, perhaps the south of France or one of the great cities of Europe. My hotel French wasn't that bad so I started to look for that unusual opportunity.

Chapter Thirteen

Pundits And Nabobs

I t was January, 1955. It was cold and damp in London and continually drizzling rain. I was definitely bored so I decided to give Alfred Marks another go. After waiting for about half an hour I was ushered to the desk of a sweet old lady who had been at Marks for many, many years. I told her I was looking for a hotel that could use a brilliant young budding hotelier, preferably an exotic resort where there were beautiful women, warm beaches and the type of wages that would allow me to support a lifestyle to which I had become accustomed. She suggested a job as a comedian in a holiday camp. I was glad at least someone had a sense of humor. As a matter of fact, I did have good credentials. Everywhere I had worked I had left with excellent references most of which were given freely. I sat and watched the sweet old lady going through the toilet rolls, which were really lists of employment positions. "How about Yorkshire?" she asked. "I have an assistant manager's position in a two-star hotel."

"Boring," I said. "Then how about working for Lyons Corner

Houses as a supervisor in one of their restaurants?" she suggested. J. Lyons was the largest catering company in the world with restaurants in every center of any consequence in England. They were also importers of tea and ran the Regent Palace and Cumberland Hotel. I replied, "Lions may be exotic, but Lyons was certainly not."

She replied, "You are a bit fussy for a young man." But she continued to look. All of a sudden she said, "I may just have the cat's whisker," whatever that meant. She went into a little file cabinet on her desk asking at the same time if I spoke any foreign languages. I replied that my grandmother had specifically taught me that "if one spoke loud enough anyone can understand English." She then asked, "How does Delhi sound?" I said, "Delhi what, as in delicatessen or as in Delice, which is a certain kind of marvelous pastry." She answered with smile, "How about Delhi as in India."

"My God," I said, "now that's exotic! Tell me more."

"Well," she said, "There is a wonderful hotel called the Ashoka Palace, small, about 150 rooms. They need an energetic assistant manager, strong in administration and food and beverage who will live in for twenty pounds a week. The company will pay the airfare one way. You will need papers, which we can help you fill out. They would like someone to start as soon as possible."

Inja, as the British pronounce it, was a little further than the south of France, but what the hell, I thought, I love curry and I did have an uncle who was a major in the Indian army and always talked about Gurkhas, Pundits and Nabobs and all that nonsense. Actually, Reg, my father's brother had showed me some great photos where he had fought with the Gurkha and was evidently quite a hero. Anyway, it sounds just "whizzo" as they in the army and I did say something about an exotic position. Just think of all those wonderful women in their saris with rubies in their navels. I looked at the sweet old lady and said, "Madam, you have just found your assistant manager. What next?" She replied, "Come back tomorrow and I will give you the papers to take over to Indian House to get the necessary documents.

That night I thought I had better pick up a quick education about India so I went into my old haunt Soho, bought a book on the Karma Sutra and had dinner at the famous Indian restaurant, Fathepur-Sikri on Germain Street. I must admit, it had an unusual smell as if no one had washed for a week and had used curry powder instead of talcum powder. It looked a bit tacky but I ordered the specialty of the house, a lamb curry. The waiter, who was Pakistani, asked if I wished it mild or hot. "Hot, of course," I said, intimating I was an old India hand and putting on my best colonial accent. I added, "And I will have a beer with it please." So this was going to be my first taste of India and Christ was it hot. I drank four bottles of beer with the curry, sweating out at least three of them. If I hadn't been quite drunk, I would have thought that my mouth was never going to return to normal. Was I going to have to eat this every day? Was I going to be able to hold up my end of the old empire?

The next day I experienced my first taste of Indian bureaucracy. I arrived at India House with my papers picked up from Alfred Marks guaranteeing a job and a half a dozen other documents and my British passport. I waited for about an hour during which no one seemed to be doing anything. Finally my name was called. An official looked at my papers and said simply, "Come back in a fortnight." "In a fortnight?" I answered incredulously, "That's not possible. I must report to my superior immediately. It's a matter of national emergency, your tourist business is in total disarray. India calls! Your country needs me."

He said, "I am much too busy to process applications." So I asked, "What about all those people with their feet on their desks? Could we call upon any one of them for help?" "Quite out of the question," he said. At the back of him on the wall was a poster proclaiming that visitors and tourists to India were honored guests. I pointed to it, slipped him five pounds and said, "Is this any way to treat an honored guest?" He turned around, looked at the poster, put the fiver in his pocket, gave me a big smile and said, "Come back after lunch." I thanked him profusely, smiling with all my charm and thinking to myself, "It's no wonder the British run India."

I visited my father two days later having spent two nights in Mayfair with Pamela, my friend from the Café Bleu, just in case I never saw my mother country again or, for that matter, a white woman. She was very sympathetic after I told her that I was being transferred to India to work in a monastery as a friar in the kitchen. She had taken two evenings off from work so to speak and we had a ball. In fact, I thought it would take six months of solitude to recover.

I must say my father was a little surprised. "India," he said, "your grandmother will have a fit" and asked if I knew anything about India. "Funny you should ask," I said. "No, how far is it from London?" He said, "By car or plane?" "Anyway," I said, "it sounds fantastic and I'm off to the land of the Taj Mahal." My grandmother, true to her word said, "Why on earth do you want to go live with those filthy people? They never wash or cut their hair." I said, "Nan, that's what you used to say about me." She was very upset to think that I was to be so far from home and British civilization. I said, "Nan, your son was a hero in Inja and now your grandson goes to achieve the same." I was leaving the country and was excited about it. My father and brother came to see me off at the airport the following weekend.

I left London in a packed Air India plane that somehow resembled a cattle car. It was full of women and children in robes and veils. The kids were all over the place dropping food and spilling drinks on the seats while their mothers just sat and smiled at each other. I learned they were Arabs on their way to Cairo which was one of the stops on the way. In Cairo most of these people got off and I visited the airport, sitting for a while in the lounge amongst the throngs of Arabs swathed in thick robes despite the incredible heat. I was drinking beer, watching the passing scene with fascination and astonishment.

I re-boarded and after nearly 14 hours of flying we arrived in Delhi. The airport was a seething mass of humanity even at 1 a.m. in the morning. It appeared that Indians travel with four or five children, also grandmother and grandfather plus aunties and uncles. The airport seemed to be packed with families either coming or going. While I was waiting for my baggage I made the mistake of going into the men's washroom. The smell was simply atrocious. As I came out an attendant handed me an absolutely filthy towel and asked me for baksheesh, which I later found out was a tip. Everyone asked for money or baksheesh. I gave him a tip by suggesting he use Tide for his next wash, a proposal he didn't appreciate. He followed me around the airport yelling at me until I gave him a British shilling which I later found out was enough to keep him in luxury for a week.

My bags arrived and incidentally they were probably the only bags on the airplane. Everything else seemed to be in large cardboard boxes or sacks tied with string. All of a sudden, I noticed a tall bearded character walking around with my name chalked on a blackboard, so I made myself known to him. He picked up my bags and with a smile he said, "Follow me, Sahib." I liked that. I thought, to hell with the filthy washrooms, if they called me Sahib, which I understood to be master, India couldn't be that bad. When we stepped out of the airport it was about 2 a.m. in the morning, but the airport was as busy as any airport in Europe at the rush hour. The night seemed to have a red glow everywhere and an incredible, acrid smell which made your eyes smart and seemed to be a combination of strong spices, those that make up curry and the pungent stench of peoples bodies. It was an incredible combination and, surprisingly, I found it quite exotic. I later found that the acrid smell also contained the smell of burned, dried cow dung, which is used as a substitute for firewood. Wherever you go, this smell follows you.

We got into a three-wheeled taxi, a sort of motorized bicycle with a cab on the back for two people. The driver immediately started to drive into town like a kamikaze pilot. By the time we reached the hotel, it was 3:30 a.m. and I was thoroughly exhausted. I was escorted immediately to my quarters which turned out to be a nice two bedroom suite and I promptly got into bed and slept for nearly 26 hours.

When I awoke I had no idea where I was and was surprised to find out that it was 7 a.m. the next day. There was a note for me to meet with the manager at 8 a.m., so I bathed, dressed, opened the door and walked out of the room, immediately falling over someone who was sleeping in front of the door. A good start. I asked him what he was doing sleeping in the hallway in front of my door and he immediately said, "Sahib, I am your servant and will cater to your every desire and wish." He immediately rushed into the room moving everything around the room at least twice into different positions. I suggested he wait outside the room until I talked to him later. It turned out that he was not an employee and had nothing to do with the hotel. He just hoped I would give him money or use him as a servant. He became an absolute nuisance and I had to have him thrown out of the hotel on several occasions. Just when I thought I had got rid of him, after having been out drinking the night before I opened the door and again fell over him. It's amazing that all you really needed to do was pay him about 10 cents a day and he would sleep outside your door for 24 hours. But apart from anything else, he stank and stopped the cool draft from coming into the room, so he had to go.

I was at the manager's office promptly at 8 a.m., foregoing breakfast even though I was starved, so as not to be late for my first meeting. He turned up at 9:30. I was to find out later that nothing was ever done on time in India. The manager was, of course, Indian and very charming. His name was Mr. Divya Singh. He was about 50 years old and previously had been a government employee in the Department of Agriculture. He was given his present position by his cousin, a high official in the government. He had also given jobs, as far as I could make out, to 10 or 12 additional cousins and other relatives. Nepotism in its highest nabobian form was typical. We went on a tour of the hotel which I found very foreign to me. For the first time I wondered what the hell was I doing in India and whatever happened to Soho, Pamela and my opera singer?

We arrived at the main kitchen and I was introduced to the chef who was Pakistani and of the Buddhist religion. The chief pastry chef and his assistant were Muslims. In the restaurant where a Cabaret was held, there was a Pakistani chef who was a Christian and so were all of his staff. The cooks who specialized in European cooking in one of the restaurants were from East Pakistan and were either Christian or Buddhist. The Indian cooks specialize in the cooking of their own region or religion only and the Muslim cooks, in Muslim cooking. Each cook had a limited knowledge of cooking of a certain district and it is not unusual when the chef gave an order to one of his cooks, to be told, "I've never heard of it." In one corner of the kitchen, they specialized in Tandoori cooking and only cooks that specialized in this work are employed in this part of the kitchen and they cook their foods in huge brick or stone and clay ovens.

It was all very confusing but important to learn that there is a caste system. India in those days had over 50 million people, today its more than 70 million, with 14 officially recognized languages, Hindi being the most used. God, what was it the little old lady said in Alfred Marks about speaking foreign languages? To be of a certain caste you had to be born into it. The manager carefully explained to me the various castes in order of prestige and wealth. The Brahmans came first, nothing to do with the Boston specie. They were the priestly caste, sometimes called apanda. Next was the Kshatriyas, who were warriors and earthly rulers with these marvelous beards and mutton chops. The doorman of the hotel was a great old man who was a Rajput Warrior from North India, even though he was seventy he was still quite fearsome to look at. Next were the Vaisyas, the merchants and artisans. The Sudras who are the servant at the bottom of the list are the untouchables or the Panchamas. Now on top of that, when you realize that people of one caste are not allowed to touch or be touched in the presence of others, you have, as they say in the hotel business, a real cast of characters.

From the kitchen, we went through the dining rooms and guest rooms. It was a very nice hotel, a little seedy but very nicely decorated and very British. The manager explained that things were a little disorganized and that we were to have a meeting with a woman who was the head of the India Tourist Company that owned and ran the hotel. The meeting would be at 9 a.m. I looked at my watch and politely said that it was nearly 10:15 now, to which he replied, "Then she will be arriving very soon." At 10:30 a.m. I met Mrs. Desai who spoke impeccable English and informed me in front of the manager that the hotel was a management disaster. From that point on, the manager wrung his hands a lot, sweated a lot and smiled incessantly.

I was informed that the hotel had 420 employees and since it was an Indian custom to never employ one man if his work can be done less efficiently by two or more, we were to employ another hundred or so employees, while cutting the payroll to keep the costs in line. That's not exactly what she said, but that is essentially what it turned out to be.

I spent the next few days dealing with each catastrophe, chaotically, one at a time. I had never seen so many employees in one place. Everyone called me Sahib and ran around me like a bunch of maniacs. Remember, I was only just 20. Admittedly, I looked much older and more so as each day went by. At the end of the week I decided that the whole thing was worse than a Gilbert and Sullivan Opera and that I had to get organized. There were just so many employees and they were driving me mad. As an example there were seven elevators. Unfortunately, they were only about 4 feet and 4 feet and each one held four people. I had decided in order to assign as many people as I could to jobs, that one man would operate the elevator even though it was automatic and that no porter would carry more than one bag at a time. Great. When you arrived with your wife and three bags, one elevator operator, two bell men and your wife would go up to your room in one elevator and the husband would arrive with his safari in another elevator, if he was lucky, 15 minutes later. I decided to take a leaf out of my uncle's army days and called reveille at 8 a.m. Monday morning. I arrived clip board in hand having previously asked personnel to assemble 100 general hands ready for assignments. Over the weekend I had made a list of all the problems that needed to be taken care of. The hotel was dirty and totally disorganized and I was full of vim and vigor. So off we set, me and my very large entourage. I felt like a mountain climber with a long line of Sherpas. We started at the front desk with me barking orders. You and you take this oil and rub the wood. You and you, this marble cleaner and clean the marble. You clean that gilt mirror to which they all replied, "Yes, Sahib. Thank you, Sahib. Thank you," bowing and running around in circles, through the lobby, into the conservatory, on into the ballroom, two by two, just like Noah's Ark. The only thing that was disconcerting was that every 10 to 15 minutes I had to leave my entourage to make quick visits to the toilet, the local food was taking some time to get used to and the only problem was the whole entourage of crazy, bowing Indians would run after me thinking that I suddenly had an emergency, which of course I did. When I explained to them what the problem was, they all thought it was very funny.

By noon I had assigned some 35 jobs and I was exhausted. It finally took me 7 days to get everyone of the first group working. Next, I took another group and set about cleaning the rooms. After about 3 or 4 weeks the place was starting to at least look clean and I was starting to go a little crazy because I was now coming full circle on myself and finding the same porter was cleaning the same gilt mirror four weeks later. Of course I hadn't told him to do any differently and I was now to find out that I had created a life long craft to be taken up by the sons and the sons of sons. It was totally ludicrous to try to organize such a large crowd of people. To some extent it was both demoralizing and exhausting. I had worked solidly for five weeks without a day off. The hotel was taking shape and I had hardly seen anything of the manager, but he had been told to stay out of the way, so he simply disappeared.

I decided it was time for some relaxation and I realized that I didn't even have a beautiful woman to go out with. However, I did know where to find one. So, first things first, tourism was certainly not a big industry in those days, but a few American tourists would come in late at night and stay one day on their way to Hong Kong or Australia and then leave the following morning. Most planes either arrived or departed at ungodly hours of the morning, like 1:00 or 2 a.m. It was also necessary to pay your hotel bill in the local currency – rupees. You were not allowed to pay it in American dollars. So, many times an American would depart at 2:00 in the morning only to find out that he could only settle his bill in rupees. Then, much to his surprise, the desk clerk would simply say, "Follow me, sir and we will change it at the bank." The guest, a little surprised, would follow the desk clerk around the side of the front desk. There was a glass door with the name of the bank on it. Everything was black inside and it was obviously closed. The desk clerk would then hammer on the door or kick the door and the lights would go on. Two or three Indians would spring up from sofas or chairs where they had been sleeping, turn on the lights and open the bank for you. This was all very confusing to the tourist, if not a little comical.

As I toured the hotel on my daily rounds, I had noticed a very beautiful woman working in the bank at a large ornate desk. She was obviously an assistant manager or someone of authority. The question was whether she was an untouchable or touchable so I decided that I would talk to her about making a deposit or something. She was dressed in a very graceful gold and green sari. She also had a spot in the middle of her forehead, which I assumed was of religious significance. As she later told me, it was purely decoration and matched her fingernail polish. She was extremely polite and had this singsong voice that sounded almost Welsh. She informed me that she had seen me around the hotel and said that she was pleased to meet me. I decided to invite her for lunch and she agreed. Her name was Indira. At least that was easy to remember. So far so good.

The restaurants and food and beverage were my responsibility but, I had become so involved in the front of the hotel and cleaning the place up that the food and beverage had been put on the back burner. As for personal eating habits, for two or three weeks I alternately had one meal and one bottle of medicine and a trip to the toilet in between. But I soon discovered that the hotter the curry, the better it seemed to kill the germs and I was now actually starting to enjoy the food.

I was also learning something about Indian cuisine. The first surprise was to see how curries were made. Unlike in the western part of the world, curries have very little gravy or liquid, certainly not even enough to cover the meat and many of them are served totally dry. Rice is served on a separate dish, and one can have it boiled, fried or mixed with sliced fried onion, fried almonds, or maybe both. You can also have a Kedgeree which is a mixture of rice and dhal cooked together usually in equal quantities. A sauceboat of unstrained boiled lentils or split peas which with the dhal is served with all the curries. Chutneys are numerous and are made fresh daily.

As time passed I got acquainted with the various chefs who showed me their own special methods of making curries from different regions. The spices with which curry powder or Masala is made is very interesting. Some spices are pounded dry, others are soaked in water or vinegar and ground to a thick paste. The curries are numerous and the spices differ, north and south of course have their own special tastes.

Tandoori cooking is another specialty. Chicken is cooked in ovens made of bricks, stone or clay and only cooks who specialize in this work are employed to do so. Obviously, one has to have a good stomach. It is also interesting that the old British colonials pride themselves on eating curry hotter than the Indians do.

During lunch I asked Indira what I should see first in India on my two days off to which she replied, obviously, the Taj Mahal in Agra a few hundred miles north. I asked her where I could find a beautiful guide who could speak English as well as she did. She smiled, lowering her eyes and said she would be delighted to accompany me. She suggested we fly and have a driver pick us up at the airport. A good hotel to stay in would be Lauries, and she would see to the arrangements. I could see she was obviously shy and reserved.

Flying to Agra was an experience. As we approached the airport at Agra enjoying the view, the hostess came around pulling blinds down and informing us that if we looked out of the window we would be reported to the captain. Supposedly, we were in a high security area. God knows why. When we alighted from the plane there was nothing in sight other than an old concrete runway and some very obsolete aircraft.

The Lauries Hotel was charming with a wide verandah across the front. It was quite crowded with American tourists who constantly stared at my companion and myself. I must admit she was a striking female, very tall for an Indian, with long hair, very fine features, and absolutely gorgeous saris in reds and golds. The room was booked in my name and little Indira had made sure of a double bed. Life was going to be just fine.

It was about 4 in the afternoon and in the lobby tea was being served, all very civilized. Outside, a snake charmer was performing on the driveway. It was like a romantic Indian novel. Indira informed me that the most impressive time to see the Taj Mahal at its most glorious was at night, so she made arrangements for the driver to pick us up at 8 p.m. She said that during the day you were plagued with beggars and although the Taj Mahal was spectacular inside, it was not sensational and outside was spectacular and that this particular night, which was almost a full moon, would be a very special experience.

We had a great dinner and I ordered a bottle of wine for which I found out you had to present a special permit. In fact, the only people who could drink legally were alcoholics and in order for me to drink, I obtained a card from the hotel doctor saying I was a registered alcoholic. I was surprised to find out that Indira did not drink alcohol, she insisted that she enjoyed all the pleasures of life that could be provided and didn't need a drink to dull her senses, very poetic and very practical. Actually, she was a Muslim and no Muslim drinks any alcohol.

The Taj Mahal is situated on the banks of the River Jumna and is certainly a sight to be seen. I am not going to elaborate on it since this is not a travel guide, but it is true that if you do see it during the day, you must also see it at night. When we arrived, the whole scene was absolutely mind boggling. A slight mist was rising from the river beyond and drifting in wisps about the garden and the Taj itself was drenched in a sort of silver light. There were a number of small parties being led around by the Indian guides who insist on coming up to you and telling you they will take you somewhere special and different to view the Taj Mahal. In fact, they really can. They can take you off to one side and show you a view of the Taj Mahal which is entirely different from the view of standing directly in front of it. They would also take you and show you the semiprecious stones that are imbedded into the walls and catch the light. From certain angles the whole wall seems to sparkle with these jewels. The whole scene was really incredibly theatrical. We walked around and sat watching as the light changed with the clouds for almost an hour. The night was quite chilly, but it was just so overwhelming that we did not want to leave. There are huge marble screens around the base of the Taj Mahal which throw off shadows. There is a huge lamp which hangs in the middle of the Taj Mahal over the tomb that sways gently in the breeze, casting a sort of ghostlike feeling. Indira explained to me that the lamp was a gift from Lord Curzon when he was Vice Regal of India.

Another exotic time to visit the Taj Mahal is in the early morning when again the mist rises off the river and it looks as if the Taj Mahal is floating in a cloud of cotton wool. This I did many years later.

We spent the morning in bed having a breakfast of exotic fruits and sweet buns and strong coffee. I decided that I didn't even want to return to see the Taj Mahal in the daylight since I think it would have ruined the fantasy that I had firmly in my mind. Later that day we returned to New Delhi. As our taxi approached the center of the city I decided I needed to go to my bank which was at Connaught Circus. Like most buildings in Delhi it was either decaying or being renovated and in this particular case it was being renovated. There was a big sign which said, "Work in Progress – Enter through Backside." English as it is spoken.

I had now been in India for about eight months. I was enjoying it, but at the same time it was very depressing. I hated the contrasts between the very rich and the very poor. I was also disturbed by the Americans, French and British who had supposedly come to India to be spiritually enlightened but were taken with the drug scene and wandered around the streets of New Delhi looking like the dregs of the earth. On one hand, I had a great companion in Indira. She showed me the real India. For instance, we went to Benares for a long weekend and to visit Benares is a very strange experience.

The daily ceremony at dawn, which is a must-see, has totally shocked some foreigners, particularly Americans who have simply called it grotesque and unnatural. It has, in fact probably embarrassed people more than repelled them. It really is uninhibited, perhaps incomprehensible in a manner altogether too exotic to accept comfortably. To see this ceremony one must get up at 5 a.m. in the morning and take a boat trip to await dawn along the great three mile eastward facing curve of the Ganges. At this time of the morning a sort of eerie mist hovers on the bank and as it clears you see high above the bank the wonderful palaces of the Maharajas and temples of at least a dozen different religions and sects. Every morning literally thousands of Hindus, pilgrims and residents of Benares stand on the ghats, which are steps leading down to the river. Some are immersed to their shoulders in this considered holy river, some allowing the water to just lap at their feet. The women are in brightly colored saris. Some of them are dressed in widows white; they wear white rather than black. Some men are either naked or wearing the briefest of loin cloths. But all of them are facing the rising sun praying as it comes up over the horizon. At the same time they make their offering of flowers or food, throwing garlands of marigolds or pink lotuses into the river. Some float small oil lamps on its surface on a sort of little boat and they take the ritual drink of the Ganges water in cupped hands and then fill a container to take with them to their temple for their religious observance. But while all this is going on, it is not uncommon to see a dead body being cast into the Ganges after having been cremated or you might see a dead cow floating down the river with its entrails hanging out and birds feeding on it. There is no doubt that its difficult to balance the dirt and squalor and the decay against the multitudes of pilgrims that come to the steps each day. However, it was a wonderful experience. In the evening I would end up back in the hotel with Indira and start another wonderful experience.

One unexpected pleasure that developed, because the hotel under my management was financially improving and running very well, was the Indian government decided to put some money into the hotel to refurbish it and I had been given the assignment to supervise all improvements. It was not that difficult since the architecture in the hotel was really great. It was just a matter of following on where the original architect had left off. There were great craftsmen around the area who could do marvelous gold leafing and carving. They were slow but they were very good. There were also great sources for carpets, tapestries and fine porcelain. I soon learned how the finest of Indian carpets were made. Unfortunately they were made by children between the ages of 5 and 8 years old, simply because only they could get their hands between the threads on the loom and, as the owner said, they were supporting a family on their paycheck. You could also order any color, size or shape.

I became quite the interior designer. I am not sure where this talent came from since I had never done any redecorating before and I must admit Indira had impeccable taste. She was a great help in telling me what was and was not the custom or appropriate in a certain area. Indira incidentally lived in a magnificent house with her parents. Her father was over 6 feet 5 inches in height and wore wonderful silk turbans. He owned an office building and was an administrator of some old trusts.

As well as the guest rooms, I was also changing the two restaurants. One was a lot of fun. I came up with a concept that transformed the room into what one imagined an Indian British Officers Club should look like, adorned with elephant tusks, palms, brass tables, oriental screens. We used leather chairs that we already had that were big and tufted. People sat and said they expected to see the Maharaja enter on his elephant. It was the old British empire look of an era long gone. These projects as well as the day-to-day operations had kept me so busy, I had not realized the year had passed so quickly. As I was sorting out some papers, I realized my work permit was expiring in two months. I was sure it wouldn't be difficult to get it renewed but, I could not see myself spending another year in India. It was really much too depressing. Everything around was decaying whether it was the buildings, the people or the machinery. Yet, I really didn't have any inclination to return to England.

As it usually happened, a decision was made for me. I was in my office one morning about two weeks later when my secretary, Nim, announced that there was an oriental gentleman representing a Hong Kong Bank, who very much wanted to meet me. I of course agreed and a very attractive, tall, gray haired Chinese businessman was ushered into my office. He told me that he had been staying at the hotel on and off for business reasons for two to three years and he could not believe the incredible changes that had taken place. In particular, the employees were so efficient, at least by Indian standards, and he was very impressed with the new look in the restaurants and guest rooms. He thought it was very elegant and showed a lot of style. He had also been informed by local residents that I was responsible for this program and wanted to compliment me. He also mentioned that he was most surprised to see how young I was, which I was pleased to hear because I thought by this time I looked at least about 70. I thanked him for his compliments and he asked me if I would care to join him for lunch, to which I agreed. There seemed to be something else on his mind. During lunch he asked me if I had ever been to Hong Kong to which I replied, no. He explained that his bank owned a very elegant hotel in Hong Kong and they were considering some renovations. They were looking for someone to be a Project Coordinator, someone who was preferably British because they had British engineers and architects working on the project. They needed someone who knew the operations to be able to coordinate with the general manager and wanted to discuss the possibilities of my joining the hotel. It was something that may take up to a year. The salary could be discussed and there were accommodations available in the hotel. His company would also pay the airfare one way. I had a feeling I was on a one-way trip around the world and not necessarily in a circle. I said that I thought it sounded most interesting, but would like a little time to consider it. In my usual impulsive fashion, I finished my coffee and said I would love to join his company and come to Hong Kong, asking "What is the timing?" He answered, "As soon as possible." That seemed to be the password of my life but we agreed one month from this particular date. I asked the name of his company's hotel and he replied, "The Peninsula."

CHAPTER FOURTEEN

Hong Kong

I was, to say the least, ecstatic about going to Hong Kong. It had always been one of those mysterious far off countries that one fantasized about visiting. Exotic food, exotic women and lots of intrigue – all the ingredients of an interesting adventure. Don't forget this was the late 50s. It's one thing to visit a country for a few days or even a couple of weeks; it is another kettle of fish living somewhere for a year or so. I hoped my new job was going to allow me some freedom and time to see this new and exciting country. I also realized it was December and that I was going to spend Christmas in Hong Kong so I decided to fly first class from New Delhi to Hong Kong. The flight was quite uneventful, food and service were excellent. One thing that was fascinating was a bowl of 10 different varieties of fruit, none of which I knew or recognized. Luckily it was served with a place mat that gave me the name and the method of preparation for eating.

The fruits were from China, Bangkok, Thailand and different parts of India and even New Zealand. I can only remember a few. One was a passion fruit from New Zealand, which is a purple fruit that you cut open and eat the contents with a spoon. The center was a puree with lots of small black seeds and was absolutely delicious, a very pleasant acidic flavor. I did try all the various fruits and it was a sensational experience. Now all these and many others are now common-place. It appeared I was entering a whole new world.

Arriving in Hong Kong was quite a surprise. I am not sure what I expected, but I don't think that I visualized Hong Kong as a mountainous island or so modern and built up. The skyline was more like how I imagined Manhattan with lots and lots of high rise buildings. It was an absolutely incredible sight. We landed not on the island of Hong Kong but on the mainland in Kowloon. Even landing was quite an experience. We flew into a bay with mountains on both sides and the airport runway was like a huge superhighway that suddenly ended where the water started. This was Kai-Tak Airport, now of course there is a new airport.

After arriving at Kai-Tak and not knowing where anything was, I decided the simplest thing was to take a taxi to the Peninsula Hotel. Actually, it turned out to be quite close to the airport. I was very impressed as we drove up to this seven-story grand hotel in sort of a U shape, facing the harbor and Hong Kong proper. Later I found out it was built at a cost of some 2 million dollars, not a great deal of money in American terms, but with the cost of labor in Asia in the 1920's, it was obviously a sumptuous palace.

Originally the hotel was to be opened in 1927 but just near completion the Civil War broke out in China. Britain was very concerned about the outcome and rushed their troops to Hong Kong. The only place that could be used as a barrack was the Peninsula Hotel. In fact, the Coldstream Guards and the Devonshires remained in the Peninsular Hotel until 1928. It must have been quite a sight, since to belong to any of these regiments you had to be a minimum of six feet tall and it certainly must have made an impression on the local

Chinese. Finally, the hotel opened in December of 1928. Now, I was to arrive 28 years later. Strangely enough the hotel was not as elegant as I had heard, but then that is why I was there since it was going to be refurbished.

The Pen, as the old staff called it, was situated on Salisbury Road in Kowloon. For years the end of the British world and the China Seas, it was sort of seedy oriental extravaganza, obviously very majestic. The rooms were large and the suites of truly imperial proportions, no doubt a "Colonial Grande Dame." Well brought up and very demanding.

I was expected and shown into a small room on the sixth floor at the back of the hotel, not overlooking the harbor, but it was still very nice. The next day I was met by someone from Hong Kong Shanghai Hotels and introduced to the rest of the team that was working on the hotel.

It was a little disappointing to find out that the decisions regarding the décor and furnishings had already been made. My job was simply to coordinate the arrival of the various furnishings and see that the rooms were installed and put back in order. Everyone thought it was important because I had experience with operations and could coordinate this with the management of the hotel. After my disappointment had faded a little, I realized that it was probably just as well. It certainly would give me more time to explore the city and get to know the area around Hong Kong. It was almost a 9 to 5 job and unlike being in operations, it got to be quite a cushy situation. After a few days working around the hotel, the first thing that dawned on me was that everyone was Chinese. This might sound a bit stupid, but I really could not communicate with anybody and half the time I couldn't even make myself understood. I was really a fish out of water. The only people that I could mix with were the architects and the Engineers and they seemed to spend most of their time drinking. Because I was living at the hotel, I was allowed to move around freely and have my meals in one of the restaurants called the Verandah. It was very pleasant overlooking the harbor. There were also two other restaurants that I could dine in if I paid for my own meals, one being a restaurant called Gaddi's, a very fine French restaurant and the other a restaurant called Chesa which looked like an English pub. It served European food with a lot of Swiss specialties. The Verandah suited me fine. It had both Western and Chinese and it was here that I started to get my first introduction to real Chinese food. Obviously, totally different from anything I had seen previously, it was a marvelous experience.

One advantage was that I had plenty of staff to work with because labor was cheap. We were stripping down the rooms getting them ready for new carpets and furnishings and starting to plan the various layouts, taking advantage of the good views. I had been in the hotel about a month when I ran into my first experience with Chinese customs. While working out some of the furniture layouts, one or two of the members of the Chinese staff who had a good understanding of the English language asked me if I had shown the furniture layout to the Feng Shui man, to which I had replied that I didn't even know who he was or what he was. They explained to me that he was a fortune teller, a kind of secular priest, part psychiatrist and almost the family doctor. Unless he gave his blessing to the rooms, they would not set them up. A little astonished, I asked how I would contact such a man. They told me they would arrange it. A few days later a strange old Chinese gentleman, who looked to be in his 90's, appeared at my door. He asked if he could inspect the rooms with me, to which I agreed happily. As we walked, he explained that first the bed must be in line with the paths of the spirits. The mirror must not face the door otherwise it would drive the benevolent spirits away. He was obviously quite serious and the employees were certainly taking him seriously, running around agreeing with him all the time. Since his ideas were not that bad and the rooms could be laid out in this fashion, I thought it better to humor him. He came two or three times a week for the next three or four months to see that I was carrying out his wishes. He then asked for a consulting fee and, after consulting with my superiors, it was duly paid.

On my days off I was starting to take the ferry across to the main island of Hong Kong which I found to be an anachronistic mixture of British colonialism and the Chinese way of life, a true melting pot of millionaires, mansions and unbelievable slums. Hong Kong is totally insufficient in food and water and it has no oil. On the other hand, it is a magnificent tropical island and a marvelous place to explore. One thing that used to drive me absolutely crazy was all the young kids and beggars who were always trying to sell something. They would just never leave me alone. However, that was soon corrected when after meeting a famous gentlemen by the name of Billy Tingle at the Hong Kong Cricket Club who taught cricket to all resident English boys. He advised me to simply roll up a Chinese newspaper in my pocket and carry an umbrella, since it rains frequently in Hong Kong. These two items would brand me as a colonial Englishman and the kids and beggars never would bother me. It certainly worked and I understand it still does today. The Cricket Club was "the" club in Hong Kong. So, when a gentleman who frequently came into the hotel and was a supplier of furnishings and fabrics invited me one day to lunch at the Cricket Club, I was thrilled. It was situated right next to the Communist Bank of China and I must say it was quite an experience. It was the last citadel of old colonial architecture and old colonial privileges. Another club that I also visited frequently was the Hong Kong Club with its red damask dining room where local Chinese businessmen were not even invited. It was indeed the Bastion of British social rank where anything more strenuous than a pink gin or a brandy was considered barbaric. I just loved it. After a marvelous dinner, one was served by a rotund black waiter dressed either as Nubian slave or Turkish Eunuch in a red velvet waistcoat. The local gentry would comment that this was a fast disappearing life style and an anachronism in today's world. As far as I was concerned, if that was true, then I was going to enjoy it while I was there.

One interesting character that used to frequent the Hong Kong Club was a gentleman called Sir Robert HoTung, a real Taipan. He was a Eurasian born of a Chinese mother and a European sea captain. He was evidently a multimillionaire and the chief executive officer of Jardine-Matheson & Company, one of the colony's prominent trading Hong Kong firms. He was always holding court in one of the comer tables. It was interesting to get within hearing distance and listen to the way he conducted business. Incidentally, he was one of the people who was against the local Chinese business people using the club, even though with a name like his, it seemed to be that he was more Chinese than British.

I was also frequenting a number of the local fine restaurants. Being friendly with the chefs in the kitchens of Peninsula. I was starting to learn quite a bit about the various foods and becoming quite a connoisseur. I discovered there are really four different regions or types of Chinese food. The southern style is Cantonese and which, for the most part, Americans simply call Chinese food. There is the Northern which is Peking style. Eastern is Shanghai and includes most seafood. Western is Szechwan and very hot. Like any other city, I tried to find out where the great chefs were. A number of the good chefs in Hong Kong operated as self-employed consultants. They received sizable fees from several restaurants at any given time.

They have their names displayed in front of the restaurants and are extremely well paid, sometimes even being offered shares or part ownership in a restaurant in order to keep the clientele coming. One restaurant that I used to visit frequently, because it was quite inexpensive, was the Mei-Li Chien which specializes in Northern cuisine from Shang-Tung. They had 250 different varieties of noodles, dumplings and breads. I must say for lunch the steamed white buns stuffed with meat or sweet bean paste, which are called BaoTze, are just absolutely spectacular. The Shia-Tze which are the pork dumplings, are also spectacular. The noodles are made of wheat, sesame, barley, beans and rice and come in all different shapes and sizes. One of my favorites was the Peking Duck which is basically served in Hong Kong six ways with everything but the quack. It's a special duck which is forced fed. It is highly glazed and roasted. The skin is sliced into strips and served with a plum sauce and sliced cucumber. It is served with paper thin Pao-Ping pancakes and a sort of spring onion which is like a paint brush. You paint on the plum sauce and then wrap in the pancake the duck meat which has been browned and served with bean sprouts. Then they serve the bloated liver which has been quick fried, and after that a custard made with the duck fat, and finally a soup made with the carcass and millet gruel.

Other wonderful dishes are the Huo-Qauo which is a mutton, very thinly sliced and dipped in boiling water. You then have a variety of dishes with vinegar, wine, soy sauce, coriander, pickled cabbage, Chinese chili sauce, fermented bean curd and sesame paste. You make up all your own concoctions and dip the thin mutton strips into these fine tasting and exotic sauces. Other dishes take an acquired taste, like a dish called drunken shrimp which is tiny live shrimp swimming in wine, water and ginger. The shrimp must be eaten just on the moment of drowning. I tried to acquire the taste, but the sight of all those shrimp drowning was just not appetizing.

One marvelous way of exploring Hong Kong was on foot. I would take the tram to the peak of Victoria and walk around Lugard Road which becomes Harlach Road and from these two streets you can see the whole of Victoria, the Capital of Hong Kong. As I walked around the streets, I could look up and see the incredible Taipans Palaces which were the wealthy homes of both the British and the Chinese.

They were palaces of pink and white and, for the most part, heavily guarded with dogs and guards carrying guns. On the other hand, if I looked down, I could see the incredible squalor of the slums, quite a contrast. Interestingly enough, the tram which was used to get to the top of Victoria only stops at a certain hour. I went to a couple of parties in this area. If you owned one of these magnificent homes and had a party, you had to charter a big tram to bring everybody up to the top and then they hire Sedan chairs to pick them up at the terminal and take them to the house. It's like a fantasy or something that you see in the Mikado Opera. Hong Kong really is an acrostic-mixture of British colonialism and the Chinese way of life. It's a melting pot of millionaires, mansions and unbelievable slums. It is a cross between the hanging gardens and gold roofs of opulent villas on the peak to the squalid hills of squatters and the fleets of junks and San pans that have literally housed hundreds of thousands of people. On the other hand, it is no doubt one of the most exotic places to live and visit in the world.

On my days off, I used to like to take a rickshaw at Wyndham Street which was where you got off the ferry and toured around some of the strange streets in the market area. Each one was selling its own different types of merchandise. For instance, there was Peddler Lane which was full of open air cobblers making shoes. There was Cat Street which was the home of all the jewelers. Also Wing Sing Street and Rotten Egg Street. There was Theater Lane which was full of hundreds of shoe shine boys where all the business people went to get their shoes shined. Then there was Wing On Lane where you could buy cotton and woolen materials. Then at night in front of the Hong Kong and Yaumati Vehicular Ferry Pier were all the food markets where they cooked at stalls and at night you could go around and eat strange dishes if you had the courage and didn't wish to know what you are eating. However, the food was truly delicious.

One place I used to end up, if I had been drinking at night and catching the last ferry back, was a stall opposite the ferry where they served a dish called beggars chicken. It was chicken stuffed with herbs and wrapped in lotus leaves and baked with the sediment of old wine jars. It really was an incredibly good dish. While standing there eating and watching, it always amazed me that these markets were right on Connaught Road in front of the Fire House Brigade Building because half of them must have been the worst fire hazards in the world.

I had been at the hotel now for about two months. Christmas sort of slipped by. I actually had Chinese dinner with people who turned out to be English Jews who sort of celebrated Christmas because of the children and it wasn't like being at home in England. On the other hand, New Year's Eve turned out to be a wild time in Hong Kong and I spent the evening walking around watching the festivities. I had taken to eating late at night and was delighted to learn that some new entertainment had started in the Verandah Restaurant. There had always been a band but now they had been joined by a gorgeous Chinese singer called, would you believe it, Fifi. She was incredibly exotic looking with very long jet black hair, the most perfect skin, slanted almond-shaped eyes, high cheekbones and the most sensuous mouth with perfect white teeth which was very unusual for an Oriental. She was quite tall, about 5'6" with straight legs, also unusual for Chinese.

It was love at first sight for me. For her, it took a little time, but we became good friends. All of a sudden, Hong Kong took on a different complexion. I started to see places that tourists had never seen, a mysterious side of Hong Kong, which I had been dying to experience. One night for instance we spent in Kowloon in the lesser known section which was a bar-come-shrine. A Buddha covered most of one wall. In front of the Buddha were incense sticks, smoking and glowing. The lights from the ceiling were a sort of double lamp with the inside revolving so that dragons appeared to be chasing each other's tail. The whole place sort of glowed with a strange light and the sickly smell of incense and something else that everyone seemed to be smoking. I was definitely out of place in my three-piece suit. It seemed to be that people were trying to tell me that I was not wanted. However, when Fifi explained who I was and I am not sure what she said, they seemed to ignore us. Soon on stage appeared the strangest group of dancers that I have ever seen. Remember once again, this is 1956. There were four or five girls on a small stage. One of them took all sorts of fruit, grapes, small mandarins, including a banana, into her pussy and then somehow shot it all out. The banana which went at least to the first table. In the front row a couple of local lads were shouting with enthusiasm. One of the girls smoked a cigarette, not in the usual way and another took a string of razor blades into her inner sanctum and then afterwards pulled them out very slowly.

My friend Fifii was quite disgusted and was ready to leave. Fortunately, just at the time we were ready to leave, the owner arrived. Knowing Fifi as a singer and curious about my presence, he sat down at the table with a large water pipe, offering it to us. Fifi explained that it was an insult if we did not at least take one or two puffs. He was a most peculiar looking man. One of his fingernails must have been 3 inches long. Since I decided I didn't want one of these stuck up my nose, I invited him to join us. The conversation was obviously a little strained - lots of smiling and nodding. After about 15 minutes, whether it was all these female acts going on or what I was smoking, I became nauseous and quite giddy. I suggested to Fifi that we should leave. We got up, making our bows and our nods and decided that we would walk back to the hotel to get some fresh air. I started to feel better and about half way decided to stop at a great hotel where they had a rooftop bar, a wonderful place for a nightcap. As I was sitting there relaxing, I suddenly realized that Hong Kong Harbor was alight with the glow of the San Pans and the city was magnificent. It had never looked more beautiful. I looked at Fifi who was absolutely gorgeous and very sensuous and I realized that I was absolutely stoned on something. It turned out it was opium and what a hangover I had the next morning. When I looked at myself in the mirror I looked so bad, I could have backed up a Chinese funeral.

The next Sunday the weather was beautiful. Fifii suggested that we take a trip to the new territories. She packed a wonderful picnic basket of cold duck and something to drink and we set off for Tap Mun Chau Island, which lay at the Eastern edge of the new territories. It was necessary to take a train, the Kowloon Canton Railway, which was very interesting. It passed through rolling hills and valleys for about 25 miles north to a place called Taipo, situated on Tolo Harbor. There we changed and took the Tup Man Chou Ferry which goes all around the coastline of the new territories. It nudges up to the foot of Ma On Shan, a craggy, 2500 foot peak where the Hakka Fanners offload pigs and vegetables onto San Pans since the ferry cannot put in to the harbor the second stop was Three Fathoms Cove. At all times the passengers had to load onto San Pans that come out to meet the ferry and its quite something to see them offloading their pigs, goats, chickens and children onto the San Pans and then paddling back to the mainland. It was a fabulous opportunity to see the boondocks of China. The ferry then turned south at the seaward end of Tolo Channel and traveled the length of Long Harbor between high barren hills and all along the seashore, back to Hong Kong where there were villages, one after another. The whole trip takes about six hours and on the return journey it started to get dark. All along the shore you could see the fisherman using gasoline lanterns to lure their catch of fish into a net spread between various boats. It was really quiet a sight! It was the first time that I had really seen China in its natural state. We arrived back at Taipo and boarded the train back to Hong Kong. A very exciting and interesting day.

The next day I was inspecting one of the suites that had just been newly decorated and furnished. I was placing some pictures and mirrors in their correct place just as the Feng Shui man had shown me. The suite was occupied but the guest was out, although an Amah, a personal maid, was pressing clothes, tidying the suite and generally keeping an eye on me. When the key turned in the lock and the guest arrived back I immediately apologized saying that I would return at a more appropriate time. He was an elderly Chinese gentleman and suggested that I finish what I was doing.

He then started to question me about the various renovations. He explained that he, too, owned a hotel in Macao and was also contemplating some renovations. We chatted for quiet a while and he asked me if I would like to visit him to see his hotel and maybe give him some ideas. I was to be his guest and I eagerly accepted. He gave me his business card; his name was Fu-Tak-Yam, and he owned the Central Hotel in Macao. Two weekends later was a local holiday so Fifi was not working in the restaurant. When I asked her if she would like to visit Macao and meet Mr. Fu-Tak-Yam, she said it was an incredible privilege to have been invited by him.

When I asked why, she told me that he was a notorious businessman who was very well known. Many people tried unsuccessfully to meet him. I said, "Well, let's go." We went down to board the Macao Ferry which was an event in itself.

The ferry building is in a strange area surrounded by dozens of tacky nightclubs, lots of stalls selling every conceivable item of food. A multitude of jugglers, fortune tellers, and musicians wandered about doing their thing. It was like one big circus.

We boarded the ferry and the trip to Macao did not take very long. Today, they have a hovercraft but we went over in a small ferryboat and it probably took about 40 minutes. Macao was in a Portuguese area of China. The reason for its existence, as far as those from Hong Kong are concerned, is the gambling. It turned out that the central hotel, which was a hotel and casino, was next to the Shanghai Bank right in the middle of the city. We were checked into a beautiful suite and there was a vase of flowers with a note to meet Mr. Fu-Tak-Yam for dinner that evening in the restaurant. So, with an hour or two to ourselves, we wandered the city and casinos and finally arrived back at the hotel in time to take a bath and change for dinner.

At exactly five to nine a Chinese gentleman, looking like he stepped out of a James Bond movie, knocked on the door to escort us to a private dining room that was set for about 8 people. It was the most exquisite table setting I had ever seen on a magnificent black and gold lacquered table. Every plate setting was hand painted and different. Gold and ivory chopsticks were sitting on carved ivory holders. It included fine crystal glasses and behind each seat stood an Oriental waiter, who looked as if he could demolish a pile of bricks with the side of his hand. When we arrived there were three other couples in the room, two Chinese and one British. Shortly after our arrival, Mr. Fu-Tak-Yam arrived with a very beautiful woman who I was told was his mistress. He was quite a character, obviously very wealthy. He told us during the course of dinner that he had three wives, nine sons and ten daughters. He put down his virility to smoking 8 pipes of opium a day. He had his own flag which depicted golden horns of water buffalo rampant in a crimson field. He also explained that in 1903 his son was kidnapped for ransom. The kidnapper asked for a million dollars. He refused to pay saying that he already had enough sons and wouldn't miss one of them.

The English couple turned out to be the Deputy Chief Super-intendent of Police in Kowloon. Three months later he was caught with $50,000 in cash in his car. The next day he was expelled from Hong Kong. His problem was Cumshaw, another term for kickbacks, and very common if you wanted to do business in Hong Kong. The Chinese couple sitting across from me also turned out to be most interesting. Again, the gentleman was very elderly and had a beautiful girl with him. His name turned out to be Ng Sik Ho and he was the equivalent of the Godfather in Hong Kong.

This was explained to me with a lot of reverence over coffee by the Superintendent of Police. Of course I could have asked him what he was doing at the same table with these two gentlemen but I thought better of it since I also had to live in Hong Kong for a while. The superintendent explained to me that the so-called Chinese Mafia was called "Triad." They were absolutely rampant in Hong Kong. The worst were the young kids who pricked their thumbs as a ritual to become blood brothers and then ran prostitutes, drugs and goodness knows what for Mr. Ng Sik Ho. It was a most interesting dinner, lots of talk of hotel business, gambling and who was doing what to whom, both in Macao and Hong Kong.

Fifi and I were sort of wall flowers, no one taking too much attention to us. But as we were parting, Mr. Fu Tak Yam suggested that I might like to talk to him sometime about managing a hotel that he was thinking of buying in Hong Kong with Mr. Kg Sik Ho. He suggested that I come back to Macao soon and spend the weekend so they could show me their plans. I told him that I thought that would be very exciting. I also said to myself that this was strictly a family

business and not for me. However, I had to be careful not to offend them. As it turned out, we had a marvelous weekend with a beautiful suite and our host could not have been more gracious. We were chauffeur driven all over Macao, saw several shows, and never spent a penny. It may be fun to run a hotel for these two, but I had a feeling it might be more like a Chinese laundry. So as Confucius say, "Forget it". Six months had past and we were now into the month of May. We were actually at the fifth day of May. This was the dragon boat festival which was a sight to behold. It was as we know it, a regatta. Many boats compete and 50 or more people get into one long boat. Drummers beat out the rhythm and they race across Hong Kong Harbor. It's very noisy and a very exciting time. Little children walk around selling sweet rice cakes wrapped in lotus leaves. If ever a trip can be planned for this time of the month and year, it's well worth seeing.

I also experienced another strange event in the month of May. One of Fifi's close relatives had died and she asked if I would like to go on a picnic. I was a little confused at the connection but agreed because she said it was something I might like to see. As it turns out, her relative had not just died but had passed away six years earlier. The family had rented the plot for a six year period, which had expired. We were going to a picnic in the graveyard. This might sound macabre, but it was incredible since for the Chinese it was a festive event. It turns out that at the end of the six year period, they dig up the remains of the body and polish all the bones, one by one, and put them into a bone jar. In the meantime everyone sat around having a picnic. There were about 12 of us and amongst us was a grandson. It was his privilege to hold the skull while the bones were being removed. Each bone, including the fingers were polished, wrapped in paper and marked. Every one of them is then sand papered, cleaned and a gentleman who turned out to be an undertaker then assembled them in a jar with each bone meticulously stacked starting with the feet and ending with the skull. It was, to say the least, a weird event. There were lots of families there all doing the same thing. I simply watched quietly remembering not to throw my chicken bones away after I had eaten a leg of chicken. But anyway, Fifi was right, it was an interesting day.

The hotel was really shaping up and the rooms were looking good. Although I wasn't learning too much about operating or managing a hotel, I was certainly learning what a great hotel should look like and what people really appreciate when they come to stay in a first-class hotel. I was also meeting some interesting people, visiting a lot of places and attending a lot of events around Hong Kong. I visited the old tourist attraction, the Aberdeen Floating Restaurant, which was quite a sea palace and a great restaurant. The best thing they served was the shrimp cooked in the shell doused in black bean sauce served steaming at the table. Another great seafood restaurant, one that I just loved to visit on Causeway Bay, was called Chiu-Chow. There they had giant crab claws in ginger and leek sauce and a specialty which absolutely fascinated me. As you entered the restaurant, displayed in a glass case were dozens of swallow nests costing anywhere from $3 to $75 a nest. I could never acquire a taste for this. It was the saliva that the birds excrete which was the delicacy everybody raved about. To prepare it, the nest was soaked in water overnight, so that the feathers floated to the top. The nest was then steamed in a stock and served as a soup. It was just something that I could never try. I was also shocked at some of the other dishes that one could order, such as fragrant meat, which was dog flesh, civet cats, toads and all sorts of things.

One thing I ate on one occasion, without realizing what it was, was snake. I had gone into a little restaurant one day and said that I just wanted a snack. The waiter looked at me and said, "Soup." I said, "Why not, sounds great." He went away and came back with this strange dark soup which had a fishy taste. It was not bad, but it turned out to be snake soup. He misinterpreted my request for a snack as snake. I always used to tease Fifi about the terrible things that the Chinese ate. For instance, one of their great remedies for a hangover that you can buy is a combination of powdered otter's penis, bear's gall, leopard bone and rhinoceros horn, which was meant to either cure anything or kill anything, to which Fifi always replied, "You think penicillin, which is just moldy cheese, and eating calves livers, snails and blood pudding is more civilized?" I must say she had a point. Time was racing by and I was enjoying myself but I felt that Hong Kong was not the place to grow. I wanted to settle down. I was starting to think of my next port of call. Although the renovation had been a great experience, I wanted to get back to operations. Hong Kong was a very small community with very little contact with the outside world. To be seen, one had to attend cocktail parties and business luncheons where at least you met visiting businessmen and learned what was going on in the outside world.

I had been invited to attend a reception for a group of Australian and New Zealand dignitaries and to see a film presentation of the South Pacific, mainly New Zealand and Australia. I attended and was fascinated by the beautiful countryside of New Zealand. I decided that this may be a very pleasant place to visit. In the course of the evening, I ran into a gentleman who was with the New Zealand Government Tourist Board, an Englishman by the name of Colbeck.

He told me over a few drinks that he had just taken over as managing director of a group of sensational tourist hotels. They were situated in some of the most spectacular locations in the world. He asked if I would like to come to New Zealand, where he would be more than happy to discuss with me the possibility of managing one of the hotels. Unfortunately, he didn't offer to pay my passage or guarantee me anything, but I thought it was an interesting proposition. He gave me his card and I stuck it away carefully, thinking that it might come in handy. Two or three weeks later, Fifi informed me that she was going to Japan with the possibility of making a record and asked if I would go with her. The offer was very tempting since we had become great friends, but I really didn't think Japan was a place I could go on speculation. We decided to take a long weekend and think about it. It was one of the most pleasant trips that I have ever taken in my life. We took the Hong Kong and Yaumatic Ferry to the Island of Lantau. The ferry stopped at the base of a mountain, which one could climb to reach a Buddhist Monastery called Po Lin Chi. The Monastery was inhabited by both nuns and monks, totally self sufficient living on their produce. We stayed overnight at a charming guest house. Dinner was prepared on a wood fire in an ancient smoke-stained kitchen. It was a simple meal consisting mostly of vegetables and baked fish, wonderful dumplings and fruits for desserts. It was really what I thought must be the ultimate Shangri La. We had a fabulous weekend. Somehow on returning to Hong Kong, I thought it was a perfect end to a great relationship and decided that if Fifi was taking off for Japan, that I would make the call and see if there was something available in New Zealand.

I called Eric Colbeck, the gentleman I had met from the New Zealand Tourist Hotel Corporation. He told me that there were many opportunities for good hotel people in New Zealand. It was a very new country and in great need of talented people. He suggested that I call him when I had made my plans. I decided to take the plunge.

CHAPTER FIFTEEN

The Land Of The Long White Cloud

M y first sight of New Zealand was Wellington Harbor. Wellington is quite a large city that sits on the Southern end of the north island, New Zealand being two main islands. The first impression that struck me was that there were hundreds and hundreds of wooden houses and very few tall buildings. It was very green, similar to England. Wellington seemed to be very hilly and gave you the feeling of tranquility; I was in the process of going through customs. There were only two customs officers available to clear the ship since it was a public holiday, Labor Day, and they simply let everybody go through. I quickly ended up in the streets of Wellington realizing there was not a soul in sight. I took a taxi to the Waterloo Hotel.

When I arrived at the hotel, there were no doormen. There was nobody around. It didn't seem to be a very impressive hotel. It had eighty rooms, one restaurant and about five bars. I was surprised because it was the flagship of New Zealand's breweries, a large company that boasted numerous hotels. I was later to find out that liquor in New Zealand is a big business and almost all hotels were controlled, if not owned, by one of the big breweries. Brewing itself was highly monopolistic. Apparently, the accommodations side of the business was less important than the retail sales of the liquor. I checked in, went to my room, which was very ordinary, and decided that what I really wanted was something to eat and drink. I headed down to find a restaurant and bar, only to discover that everything was closed up because it was a public holiday. It was also explained to me that the bars closed on Sundays and at six o'clock every other night. In 1893, the Alcoholic Liquor Sales Control Act was passed giving New Zealand the system which, with very few modifications, still existed on my arrival. I headed out to take a look at the city and see what I could find. The only thing open was a milk bar that sold milk shakes and sandwiches, hardly a great start in a new country. Whilst I was sitting there eating a toasted sandwich, which I understand was invented in New Zealand, someone was talking on the radio. It sounded like an auction although I couldn't understand a word they were saying. Asking the young lady behind the counter what it was, she explained to me that it was the horse races and that everybody was at the races. Well maybe what I really needed was a good sleep so I headed back to my room. I tried to buy a newspaper but was told they too were not printed on Sundays or holidays. I was not too enthusiastic about my new surroundings, but after all I was the guest of the Tourist Board and who knows what was up the road.

The next morning I placed a call to the Chairman of the Tourist Board to make an appointment. He came onto the line excitedly explaining that he had a fabulous opportunity for me. It was not with the tourist hotels and it was in Auckland, which was the northernmost tip of the north island. He explained to me that there was a very famous

New Zealander by the name of Kerridge who owned a number of theaters. He had a restaurant called the Gold Room and was looking for a sophisticated manager.

Colebeck explained he had already talked to Kerridge about me describing me as an experienced restaurant and hotel manager from England and Hong Kong. Well, it was partly true. I had certainly worked in those countries. Mr. Kerridge, he explained, was awaiting a call at my convenience. I hung up feeling a little bit put down. I had come an awful long way only to be told that there was a job waiting for me somewhere else. I hoped this wasn't going to be a bad habit.

I called Mr. Kerridge who said that he wasn't very far away in Auckland and asked, "Why don't you get up here as soon as you can?" He suggested that I take a plane the very next day and said he would personally meet me at the airport.

Upon arrival, I was to look for a1956 Rolls Royce. He would have the air tickets delivered to the hotel first thing in the morning and a car would take me to the airport. Well, I liked his style so I agreed to see him the next day.

Next morning I arose early taking breakfast at 7:30 which consisted of a table d'hôte menu. You could either have a fruit juice, porridge, steak and eggs, chops, kidneys, liver; it looked like a farmer's breakfast menu. The staff was so casual it was unbelievable. This was a different hotel business compared to the one I knew.

The car arrived promptly to take me to the airport with all my worldly possessions which fit into two suitcases. After what was nearly three hours of flying north, I arrived in Auckland. Leaving the airport building, I looked for a Rolls Royce and sure enough there it was, a gorgeous Muliner Silver Dawn in the most hideous mauve color I had ever seen. I could not believe that someone would have the temerity to paint a Rolls that color. As I walked toward the car, out stepped the famous Kerridge who turned out to be a very pleasant gentleman. On the way into the city, he explained how he had started as a railway porter and had made millions of dollars, owning many theaters in conjunction with the Odeon Company in England. Well, it certainly seemed a land of opportunity if you could go from railway porter to millionaire.

He explained that he had opened a restaurant in the city called the Gold Room that was not doing well, and it needed help. We arrived at the restaurant which was indeed opulent, if not elegant. Its decor was white leather banquettes, gold fabrics on the wall, lots of crystal and lots of mirror. A little garish, but a very modem kitchen. There was also a lesser restaurant on the other side called the Blue Room which was more like a coffee shop. The menu was good - European. The chef was Dutch. There was music at lunch with a trio and a well-known pianist by the name of Jack Thompson, but evidently Kerridge was losing a small fortune.

We had a very pleasant lunch and were joined by I think his second or third wife and a second woman who was very attractive, dressed in an elegant black dress and a large hat. I remember this well because she impressed me as quite an elegant female with one of those sort of husky voices, a little bit like Lauren Bacall. She was an actress and her name was John. I politely inquired if that was Jean. "No," she said with a smile, "just John."

After lunch Kerridge invited me to the office and we discussed the position of Manager. I explained my interest in taking the job, saying that on the surface I could not see anything wrong with the restaurant and that I had no idea why he should be losing so much money. I told him that if he would give me a few weeks, hopefully, I could come up with some answers. It was agreed and I took the job.

Kerridge suggested as a temporary solution to my living problems, I should get a room in what was called a private hotel. Similar to England, it was a hotel with no liquor license. His secretary made some phone calls and I had a place to stay. It was Thursday and I would start on Monday. As we were walking to the street, Kerridge asked me what I thought of our luncheon companion, John, adding, "Isn't he a character?" I looked at him a little bewildered as he explained that John was a very famous New Zealand female impersonator with a group call the Kiwis. I decided that I better take things a little carefully in New Zealand.

Over the weekend, I explored Auckland. It was October and summer was just starting. They had, of course, a reverse season to Europe. I thought not only was I going to spend Christmas in a new country, but in the middle of summer and probably on the beach. As I walked around the city, I realized that Auckland, although it was the major city in New Zealand and considered to be the most modern, was in fact terribly old fashioned. I soon discovered that the food was terrible, to say the least. English family-style is an overstatement, mostly lamb and mutton, steak, cut 1/4 inch thick. It was as tough as boots. However, the people were very friendly. I could see that life in a small society could be dull, but it obviously had its compensations. There seemed to be more opportunities for people to do things, as opposed to watching others do them. Sport seemed to be New Zealand's main religion. There were lots of rugby matches and everyone else went to the horse races.

It was Saturday and I was walking down Queen Street, the main street of Auckland, who was standing and talking to a small group of friends but Terri, a young lady I met on the boat. Boy, did she look good. She was as surprised and pleased to see me as I was to see her. We immediately agreed to meet for dinner. She suggested the best hotel in town, the Trans-Tasman at six o'clock. I asked, "Isn't that a little early?" To which she replied, "No, we have to get there because the kitchens close at eight o'clock, even on Saturday night."

Over dinner Terri filled me in about New Zealand and the way of life which started to sound more and more boring. I told her about the Gold Room and she was very impressed with my position, adding that it was considered to be the finest restaurant in Auckland, if not New Zealand, outrageously expensive and just a toy for Kerridge. However, there were rumors that he might close the place down, not very encouraging for my future. We had a very ordinary dinner and Terri suggested that since she had a car, we should go to her parent's home and I should spend the rest of the weekend with them, hastily adding, in separate bedrooms. It turned out that she lived in a gorgeous large ranch-style house, right on the harbor. Her father was a New Zealander, a barrister. Her mother, who was as beautiful as Terry, was part Tahitian and part French from the Caledonian Islands. They were an attractive and pleasant family. On Sunday, they drove me around the city and I must say I got an entirely different impression. It was one of the most picturesque cities I had ever seen, beautiful flowers, trees, long beaches and fabulous weather. It was a very pleasant weekend and a great start in a new city.

I started work on Monday. The first thing I did was call a staff meeting which turned out to be a very large event. Since I called it at 10:00, they served morning tea which was an elaborate affair with pastries and cakes. I asked if this was a normal event and they said that every day they had morning coffee at 10:00. It was, in fact, a tradition. There were so many assistant managers, bar managers and accountants that I couldn't understand what everybody did. I requested revenue figures, food and beverage costs, and the like. I was promptly given daily revenue numbers. No one knew what the food costs were and the chef said he simply took inventory at the beginning of the month and at the end of the month. What was used was the food cost.

The restaurant was full at lunch and half empty at dinner. It didn't take too long to show that it was a losing battle. There were simply just not enough customers and the concept was ten years too soon. It wasn't appreciated, or for that matter, understood. I presented a very professional set of profit and loss statements together with the years forecast to Kerridge at the end of November. He looked over them, thanked me and decided to close his place two weeks before Christmas. Great, I talked my way right out of a job and right at Christmas time to boot. However, the weather was sensational being of course the middle of summer, so I took a week off and spent time with Terry and her parents. After the holidays, I started looking for a job. Hotel managers didn't seem to exist. There were more publicans interested in beer sales. The hotels were very small and were more typical of mediocre English taverns.

I decided that I needed to pay rent so I applied for a job as a cook at the Station Hotel. The chef was very impressed that I had been to hotel school and immediately gave me the job. He gave me the vegetables for the next two days which were written on a blackboard, amongst them were chateau potatoes and cauliflower au gratin. I put two sacks of potatoes through the machine and turned all the potatoes into chateau potatoes, which are barrel shaped with 8 sides. I parboiled the cauliflower, squeezing the floweriest into miniature cauliflowers and napping them with a light béchamel sauce. Two hours later, I had finished the vegetables for the next two days. I told the chef, whose name was Bruce that I had completed the task. He freaked out at seeing what I had done. He had never seen anything like it and brought the whole kitchen and half the hotel in to see what I had done. He thought I was so brilliant I was appointed Assistant Chef by the end of the day.

For the next two months, I was the talk of the town. Nobody seemed to have any training in a professional kitchen. All their menus were written in poor French with the names having very little similarity to the dish.

When I started to produce good food, the restaurant started to get quite busy. After about two months, I received a call from the Trans Tasman across the road and was invited to apply for the Assistant Manager's job in charge of restaurants and bars, which I did. Two months later, the General Manager had a drunken argument with the owners and quit. Four months after arriving in Auckland, I was made the Manager of the Trans Tasman Hotel which was the largest and best hotel in the city. "Good Lord," I thought, restaurant manager to vegetable cook to general manager all within four months.

It wasn't a bad hotel, about 60 rooms, a nice restaurant, about four stories high with a commanding view of Auckland Harbor. I lived on the top floor and found the job to be very easy. A few weeks after I had been appointed Manager, I awoke very early one morning and decided to get up and take a walk. It was about five in the morning. In passing the kitchen, I heard lots of noise. I thought it strange, since I understood no one appeared before 6 a.m. I decided to see what was going on and much to my surprise, the Chef was loading trays of cooked meat pies, cakes, eggs and flour into the back of a van. The van displayed the name of a restaurant on Queen Street, which it turned out he owned and had been supplying for the last five years from the hotel. Even the two early morning cooks who were working with him were on the payroll of the hotel but later went down and worked in the kitchens of his restaurant. I kicked him out, then and there.

Two weeks later, I caught the bar manager loading two or three cases of liquor into his car for a party that he was having at his house that weekend. He, too, was promptly dismissed. Everybody in this place seemed to be doing their own thing and stealing the place blind.

On Sundays, the country literally came to a stop. None of the bars were open, shops were closed and the city was empty. There was not even a Sunday paper published. I was outside my hotel apartment one Sunday morning when I overheard a strange conversation. We had a Russian maid called Lola who was having a discussion with an American visitor from Texas. He was explaining, "There is no paper in my washroom." To which she replied, "of course there isn't, there is no paper on Sunday." "No," he said, "You don't understand, I need paper in the washroom." To which Lola replied, "I wish these Americans would understand that New Zealand has its own customs and if they don't like it, they should go back home." He immediately left looking for help from someone else.

A few months later, I was asked to meet with the Directors. Expecting some praise and perhaps an increase in salary, I was surprised at the meeting to be told that the hotel had never been run so well; in fact, it was making money after continual losses for a number of years. However, the employees were very upset with me and there was a serious morale problem. I was told that I was much too strict and that I should look for something else. I sat there for a moment, a little stunned, thinking that in less than 12 months, I had gone from the restaurant manager of a very elegant restaurant, to a cook, to an assistant chef, to a general manager to unemployment and it was almost Christmas again. I must say, I was a little pissed. I was later to learn the New Zealanders don't like conflict. A New Zealander would rather say, "Let it go mate," than to correct someone.

The next day I received a call from one of the Directors. He asked me if I would like to have lunch with him, to which I agreed. Over lunch he explained that I was just too controversial and although I had done a good job, the Directors were giving the Chairman of the Board a hard time since the hotel was finally making money. I was obviously a threat to him so he had decided that I should leave and stop rocking the boat. However, as a Director, he agreed with everything I had done and because I could weed out troubles he had something that I might be interested in. It turned out that he was a Senior Officer in an Australian Accounting Firm that had been asked to take over a hotel in Sydney, Australia. As receivers, they needed an interim manager for anywhere from six months to a year and they would be prepared to fly me to Sydney for an interview at their expense. It seemed like a pretty good idea since I was out of work and had to move out of the hotel by the end of the week, so I agreed to fly to Sydney.

Sydney was more like it, a large bustling city and its Chevron Hotel was in one of the more exciting spots called Kings Cross. It was a modem high-rise with quite a large number of rooms and several great looking restaurants. Beside the hotel was the largest man-made hole in the Southern Hemisphere, an excavation to take the largest building in Australia until they ran out of money. The city looked like fun. I enthusiastically accepted the position as General Manager Designate.

CHAPTER SIXTEEN

The Land Down Under

*S*ydney is the capital of the State of New South Wales. It is not only Australia's oldest, largest and liveliest city, but also where about 25% of all Australians lived. It really was quite cosmopolitan, something like London or Hong Kong which was to me quite a surprise.

The hotel was the Chevron. It had been a Hilton Hotel and for some reason or another, the owners, two brothers in the hosiery business, had gone into bankruptcy. On arrival at the hotel, I met with four of the Directors who represented the owners and the receiver. After a short interview, I was offered the job. Since I brought all my worldly belongings with me, it was an easy decision and I started work the following week.

The hotel really was quite busy. As I was told the problem was that the two brothers who had owned the hotel previously, or previous to it going bankrupt, had simply drained the hotel of all its cash, putting in into their hosiery business. Therefore, although the hotel was doing reasonably good business, it was continually short of cash for maintenance and other such problems.

Nevertheless, there was a nightclub called the Silver Spade that did a great business and during my tenure at the hotel we had Fran Jeffery, Frank Sinatra, Tony Bennett and other very notable entertainers. There was also a great bar on the street level called the Long Bar where all the barmaids were over 6 feet tall and wore grey silver wigs with very low décolletage-type dresses so that when they leaned over the bar and poured you a pint of beer, you got a free show. They were also very expert at sweeping any loose change off the bar with their damp bar rags. There was many a bar customer who turned around to find out that they had taken all of his loose change. But they looked at him so sweetly that he dare not create a fuss.

The hotel sat just on the edge of Kings Cross or as the Sydney-siders call it, the Cross. As I found out, living at the Cross can mean anything from Pots Point to Elizabeth Bay or Woolloomooloo. It was the most exciting area of Sydney and where most of the night spots and restaurants were concentrated. It compared to London's Soho. The hotel was quite large, more than 500 rooms. It also had the distinction of having beside it the largest man-made hole in the world. An excavation that was meant to add another 500 or 600 rooms had been completed, but they ran out of money before they could get construction under way.

The hotel itself was very busy. It was an interesting experience for me because although I could not make too many decisions or changes since my position was that of a sort of caretaker, I did have the backup of a large company to make many operational analyses. So, I literally took the hotel apart one day at a time to see what made it tick. The restaurants and bars, particularly the bars, were very busy. Being on the edge of the Cross, it attracted many locals.

On one particular day, there was cause for hilarity when a couple of out-of-towner's had an interesting experience in one of the small bars.

A gentleman, accompanied by his wife, came into the Sportsman's Bar to have a drink. His wife, having a headache, decided to go off to bed. The gentleman decided to stay and have another drink in the bar. After about 20 minutes, he also decided to retire to his room. He inadvertently left his key on top of the bar, not realizing that this was the thing to do if you wanted some female company in your room. Getting to the lobby and realizing that he didn't have his key, presumably he thought his wife had it, so he got another one from the front desk and went up to his room. Arriving at his room, his wife was already in bed and dozing quietly. He quickly undressed. He had just stripped down to his bare necessities when there was a knock on the door, the key turned in the lock and a young lady walked in, smiling, cheerfully exclaiming that he must be in a hurry because here he was already naked and she promptly stepped out of her dress. She was indeed totally naked when she realized that there was somebody else in the bed and she rather excitedly said, "Who the hell is that?" His wife, hearing some commotion, woke up, sat up in bed; saw her husband standing naked in the middle of the room and an also very nude young lady staring at her. She, in turn, said, "Who the hell is that?" It was indeed an amusing incident and the gentleman, recalling the incident the next day, thought the whole thing was hilarious and would certainly be a good story to tell for months. I understand it cost him a fur coat to get his wife to believe his side of the story.

Another funny incident that happened while I was in the hotel was at a function for Quantas, the Australian airline. They were having a dinner and reception at the hotel and as a feature entertainment; they had brought in a large red kangaroo that was to be their mascot for the evening. This kangaroo had been trained to box, not unusual in Australia and later in the evening was going to put on an exhibition with one of the local fighters. In the meantime, they had tethered the kangaroo in one of the bedrooms of a suite to keep him safe and sound until they needed him.

Someone forgot, however, to Inform hotel management. Well, when the maid entered the room to turn down the beds, she got such a fright that she ran out of the room leaving the door open. The kangaroo, having somehow slipped his tether, ventured out into the corridor and down towards the main staircase that led to the lobby. At this unfortunate time, a gentleman who was leaving one of the bars slightly inebriated came face to face with this kangaroo and thought that he might like to have a fight. He raised his hands and stated, "Put up your dukes" but, unfortunately, before he could even finish the sentence, the kangaroo had hit him with both feet sending him down two flights of stairs to the lobby and breaking his collarbone. Everybody, except the unfortunate customer thought it was very funny. I was sure we were going to see a lawsuit on our hands, but evidently he was not meant to be in the city that night, let alone the hotel, and I imagine he was a little embarrassed to tell anyone he had been punched out by a kangaroo.

Eight months had gone by after I had arrived in Sydney and finally the hotel was sold to a family who were going to run it themselves, so my job had come to an end. However, I was then asked by the accounting company to go to a hotel at Broad Beach on the gulf coast in Queensland and relieve a manager for four weeks whilst he was on vacation. Interestingly, in Australia, it was the manager who held the liquor license. The manager could only be relieved by another licensed manager if he should go on vacation. Since I had received a license when I came to Chevron, I agreed that it would be a pleasant vacation to go to the Gold coast.

As it turned out, the Gold coast was a bit garish and flashy. I imagined it to be similar to perhaps Miami in the United States. It was hot, lots of sun 290 days a year and a barrel of fun. Some of the most beautiful women I have even seen in my life were on the beaches, blond and tanned and tall. Everyone seemed to be very casual. No one wore anything but shorts or a swimsuit and at the end of four weeks, I had a great tan and felt very fit. I swam every day at Surfers Paradise, a gorgeous stretch of miles and miles of beach and surf. Because of the heat, I had become a beer drinker, starting at around 10 in the morning and finishing at around 11 at night. Just when I was wondering whether I was going to become an alcoholic or a beach bum, I was asked if I would like to go on another assignment to Melbourne in Victoria to relieve a manager at the Menzies Hotel.

I thought that was a good idea and that this relief manager business really wasn't a bad job since you get to travel, stay in the best hotels, and see the country. I was driving from city to city and seeing the countryside covering enormous distances but, because I was in the hotel for a very short time, I didn't have to make any decisions, nor work particularly hard.

Melbourne was a very cosmopolitan city, but very conservative. The city literally rolled up its sidewalks when the shops closed at 5 p.m. The hotel was a wonderful old hotel with lots of tradition and it was the type of hotel that I would like to have managed on a permanent basis. Strangely enough, it too, had some troubled times and there was talk that it was going to be pulled down and a new building put up in its place. It was a very pleasant hotel to run. One morning, much to my surprise, Terri called from New Zealand saying that the Mayor of the City Dunedin in the South Island of New Zealand was looking for a general manager for The Grand Hotel which he owned. The Mayor evidently was a friend of Terri's father and would, on his recommendation, offer me the job sight unseen. It was very tempting to have a permanent address for a while and it would be nice to see Terri again, so I agreed. At the end of my month, I traveled back to New Zealand to the city of Dunedin.

CHAPTER SEVENTEEN

Back To New Zealand

Dunedin was a very conservative city with a mixture of English and Scottish heritage. The Grand Hotel was the best hotel in the city with about a 100 rooms. It had a very busy restaurant and quite a lot of function space. It ran full most of the year and in fact was a sweet hotel to manage. It had very few problems and little need to expand business. The mayor of the city was the owner. Consequently, all the important people stayed at the hotel and all the important city and social functions were held there.

One such function was "Women of the Empire," a very staunch pro-British group. On one special occasion they had an afternoon tea for about 300 local ladies and as a special gesture, the hotel made a cake approximately 2 feet by 3 feet that was a replica of the Union Jack and all its red, white and blue glory. However, the Chef really poured in the red and blue dyes to color the flag to the point that when everyone was eating their cake, I happened to walk through the function room to check that everything was going well, and all you could see were bright red and bright blue mouths chatting away incessantly. I must say it was very comical.

The hotel ran so well and life seemed to be so pleasant especially since I met and fell in love with a young lady, Janice Price. She was a very beautiful New Zealand girl from Christchurch the only daughter of an old New Zealand family. Janice was working in the hotel on the front desk and it was love at first sight. After a month of dates we decided to get married. She duly moved into the hotel and life became very comfortable. However, as will happen many times in the hotel business, I started to get itchy feet and thought it would be fun if we both traveled around to see more of the country. Luckily, I didn't really have to look very far.

The gentleman who had originally offered me a job in New Zealand, Eric Colbeck, suddenly appeared again at The Grand Hotel and told me that one of the most magnificent hotels in New Zealand was a hotel called Milford Sounds. It was a tourist hotel deep in the heart of the mountains and the lake district of the South Island.

He offered my wife and me the position of managing this very fine hotel. Since The Grand was a nice hotel, but not very exciting, we decided that it might be fun to take off and try greener fields.

It was agreed that I would start as managing director of the Milford Sounds Hotel within one month. We were told that if we drove to a small town called Queenstown, a plane would come and pick us up and fly us into Milford Sounds, since it was 6 weeks before the season started and the roads were not yet open because of snow drifts. I had just bought a very large Humber Super Snipe. 1 thought this would be a great opportunity to try out our new car and drive down the two or three hundred miles to Queenstown, which we did in very short time. Queenstown was situated on the side of the lake and was very picturesque with mountains all around. We stayed at a small hotel and awaited the arrival of the plane to take us into Milford Sounds.

Meanwhile, we were joined by a bar manager and a restaurant

manager that had also been hired to go in at the same time. However, for two days the plane could not land because of the fog around the area and with the mountains, pilots were very careful to pick exactly the right weather to come in. I decided, after looking at a map, that Milford Sounds really wasn't very far from Queenstown and suggested that we all drive in my car, to which everyone agreed enthusiastically. So, we set off to drive the remaining 200 miles. The weather was fabulous, the sun was out, there was very little snow and we made very good time for the first 150 miles. But then all of a sudden as we started to climb into the mountain area, less than 30 miles from the hotel in Milford Sounds, we struck deep snow on the roads. Within a very short time, I was finding it very difficult to drive on the roads. But we made it within 300 yards to a tunnel that, according to the map went through the mountain. It was the called Homer Tunnel. And, there we stuck in the snow. Probably 7,000 feet up into the mountains, with snow all around us and bloody cold, and nightfall coming on too rapidly for comfort. We tried everything we could do to get the car to go up the last 300 yards, but finally gave up leaving the car in the snow and walking to the tunnel, thinking that once we were through the tunnel, we would have a short walk to the hotel.

Getting through the tunnel turned out to be a nightmare. The tunnel was a mile long and pitch black with the sounds of huge waterfalls and deep caverns all around us. We used a miserable flashlight and cigarette lighters to get about 1/3 of the way in and then ended up feeling ourselves along the wall every inch of the way, thinking that any minute we were going to drop over the side of a huge waterfall, or fall into a crevice at the side of the tunnel. We simply could not see anything. My wife was understandably fairly hysterical, and the barman was having problems as well.

Finally, after what seemed an intolerable amount of time, we made it to the other side of the tunnel and we looked out onto a huge valley of mountains and dense undergrowth and absolutely nothing in sight for miles. It finally took us three hours to walk to the hotel. We walked down the side of the mountain and reached the hotel around midnight, absolutely exhausted.

Once we told the Assistant Manager what had happened, he told me that I could not possibly leave my car on the other side of the tunnel. He said that the block would freeze and if that didn't destroy the car, it was quite possible that an avalanche would. So, a group of engineers and hotel employees, along with me and a couple of jeeps, went back up to the tunnel to rescue the car. Going up to the tunnel was not very complicated and once inside the tunnel, I realized that all our fears were really unwarranted, since the waterfall was only a small stream running along side the tunnel. But, the noise was quite deafening and more terrifying than the look of the stream. What was a little frightening was that all along the roof of the tunnel were stalactites or huge icicles that could spear you to the ground if one fell off.

Once on the other side of the tunnel, we hooked up the car to the jeep and towed it into the tunnel. Then I was off and running down the other side.

I was soon to be absolutely scared out of my wits to find out that the bridges that I had to cross were only just a little bit larger than the car and there was a shear drop of thousands of feet down either side with no barriers on the sides of the bridges. I had heard that Milford Sounds was isolated, but this was ridiculous. However, Milford Sounds is truly one of the most magnificent places in the world. Its spectacular and grand scenery makes one feel so very insignificant in the natural order of things. Situated in a deep basin, fed by the sea, its vertical cliffs rise straight away for thousand of feet from the water edge. It is a true fairyland.

The hotel sits on the lake facing a mountain that simply rises out of the middle of the lake. It is a tourist hotel and was only open for 8 months of the year. So after managing this truly glorious hotel for 8 months, the tourist department asked me if I would like to then go to a hotel on Lake Taupo. It was another magnificent hotel on the side of the lake where some of the best fishing in the world was to be found.

My great friend Curt Gowdy the Famous Red Socks commentator and Host of the American sports show, later told me he had the best fishing of his life at Lake Taupo. So since these hotels were a pleasant existence you lived in, saved all your money and basically there was nowhere to go because they were all in isolated locations, it was good for building a nest egg and my wife loved the idea of living in a famous tourist destination.

The hotel at Lake Taupo was quite an experience. We had been there about one week when it started to rain. It started to rain like you would imagine the monsoon rains in India. The skies just opened up and the rain fell out. However, it didn't stop after an hour, two hours, eight hours, twenty-four hours and we had floods like I have never experienced before. The water was coming into the ground floor of the hotel. The furniture was starting to float around and the carpets were starting to lift off the floor. Obviously, the kitchen had to be closed down because the water was getting into the bottom of the ovens.

The hotel was surrounded by a small village, totally populated by Maoris. They thought the whole thing was a bit of a joke and one by one started to disappear. I was later to find out that they had what they call a "pa" which is a big meeting house built on the top of a hill just outside the village. So the whole Maori population simply moved their families up to the "pa", took their beer and their guitars and some food with them and had a glorious party for two or three days. Meanwhile, I was left with almost no one in the hotel to do any of the work.

There were a few humorous incidents arising out of the flooding. The local Maoris had acquired two or three rowboats and would row into the car park where we were still selling cases of beer from the storeroom which we would load into their rowing boats. A not so humorous incident was a gentleman who was trying to walk across

117

the parking lot to his car which was now covered with water and he disappeared from sight. Evidently the top had floated off one of the big septic tanks and he simply disappeared from view into about 20 feet of water, later to appear, not too much the worse for wear, but not smelling too good.

After the floods had subsided, I found that I was missing half the pots, pans, silver, glassware and everything out of the hotel and the Maori's by nature never stole anything, they just borrowed things. So I took a truck and a couple of helpers, went up to the "pa" and retrieved a truck full of cooking utensils, plates, pots and pans. They basically had catered a week-long banquet up there for about 250 people.

Several months later I was sitting enjoying a drink just after dinner around 8:00 at night in the lounge with some guests, when someone came rushing in saying that the Riverside Lodge Hotel, another local inn was on fire and that they couldn't find the barman who had the keys to the fire shed where the fire engine was kept. Obviously, I looked a little startled. He then explained that the hotel had a series of volunteer employees who made up the local fire brigade along with a couple of locals.

First of all, I couldn't believe that anyone would be stupid enough to lock the fire engine into the fire station, but they said it was to stop the children from playing on the fire engine because it was left unattended most of the time. So, along with a couple of cooks, maintenance people, and my bar manager, we rushed out into the village to find where the fire station was. One of the engineers brought along a crowbar and once we found the fire hall we pried the lock off the front of the door. We then found behind it this wonderful fire red fire engine. It looked to be quite an antique, but it was magnificently polished and all equipped. Since the driver designate was not around, I took the driver seat, turned over the engine and surprisingly it started the second time around. Everybody piled onto the fire engine and on we drove out of the fire station. The only problem was that I couldn't get the damn thing out of first gear. I was double clutching. I was doing everything I thought I should do, but all I was doing was crashing gears. So we roared off down the main street of Taupo clanging the fire bell, everyone screaming at the top of their voice at about 5 to 6 miles an hour in first gear. It seemed an intolerable amount of time for us to reach the scene of the fire which was at least five or six miles down the road. When we arrived, sure enough half the hotel was ablaze. The crew immediately jumped off the fire engine and pulled out a fire pump. They connected the hoses. Two people ran with the hose towards the fire and the other members of the crew ran to the river with the pump and the other end of the hose. We stood there for what seemed to be a long time waiting for the water to come out of the hose and nothing happened. I presumed that they couldn't get the pump started so I immediately rushed down to the river to find out what the problem was. Surprise, surprise, someone had fallen in the river with the pump. It was obviously a hopeless situation. We would never get the pump started again, so we simply gave up, at which point two or three of the Maori's broke out some cases of beer. Everyone sat around, someone played the guitar and I felt like Nero drinking beer, watching the hotel bum down, but there was little else anyone could do.

Again, the season in a matter of months, started to come to a close and since my wife Janice came from Christchurch, the main city on the South Island, we decided to go to Christchurch and see if there was a possibility of me finding a job in Christchurch. Sure enough, without very much trouble I landed a job with New Zealand Breweries and took over the management of Warner's Hotel, which was situated just behind Christchurch Cathedral. And in those days, it was without a doubt, the best hotel in Christchurch, if not New Zealand.

It was an old established hotel, six stories high, about 60 rooms with a very fine restaurant, a nice bar and catered to a very nice group of people. A lot of wealthy cow cockies, as they called them, stayed there. These are the wealthy farmers who have big sheep stations with sometimes up to half a million sheep on them. Others that stayed there were the corporate traveler who traveled from Australia, overseas and major cities in New Zealand. It was a wonderful hotel and I soon started to make a reputation for being the hotelier about town. I took on a half hour radio program three times a week on food and wine. I wrote a column for the local newspaper called "The Fine Art of Living," and really started to enjoy the city life. My son, Warren, was born that year and life was very pleasant living in a hotel in the middle of Christchurch.

To put the type of client into the proper perspective, one day I was standing outside the hotel and I saw the most magnificent Rolls Royce Phantom V, by Hooper. While in the process of admiring the car, I was shocked to see in the back-seat two or three Marino sheep. Just as I was looking at the sheep, out of the hotel came a Mr. McKenzie, one of the more prominent farmers in the south island of New Zealand. A multimillionaire by anyone's standards. I explained to him that I was rather surprised to see sheep in the back of the Rolls and he carefully explained to me that, first of all, the sheep were worth more than the car. He had just bought them at an auction and he didn't think it was sacrilegious at all.

Another amusing incident that happened while I was at Warner's had to do with a very famous outback New Zealander by the name of Barry Crump. He was making a great reputation for himself having written a book that was going to be made into a movie. We were to have the premiere party in the hotel and first everyone would go to the movie theater a few doors away for the premiere of the movie.

Barry Crump was a very colorful character. He was a New Zealander that lived in the backwoods and had written a book about survival in the backwoods. For the premiere, he had been asked to say a few words to the gathering before the movie and, because of this, he had also been asked to put on a black tie and tuxedo which he had never worn before in his life. I could see that he was terribly uncomfortable and not at all at home in his new surroundings. I took him for a few beers into the bar before he had to go over to the theater. He was absolutely petrified at having to give, what turned out to be a 2-page speech that had been written by the movie people's public relations department. But finally, after pouring a few beers into him, we got him into the theater and up onto the stage along side the Mayor of Christchurch. The Mayor made the necessary introductions of the film and then turned over the microphone to Barry. At which time he absolutely froze. The Mayor tried to prompt him and nothing came out. Suddenly, he let it all come out in his backwoods New Zealand accent. "What can I tell you mates? It's a fucking great movie and you should watch it." The audience went wild and gave him a standing ovation.

New Zealand was becoming quite a tourist center. Suddenly visitors were discovering the beauty of the islands and the first new hotel for 15 years was going to be built on an international golf course just outside of Christchurch. It was going to be a magnificent hotel. It would be considered a small hotel by today's standards, about 100 rooms, with the ability to add on more rooms if the necessity arose. It was on an international golf course and it had been designed by New Zealand architects who had won awards for building churches. The result was a rather interesting Japanese style hotel with lots of wood, low roofs, dry river beds with white boulders and beautifully landscaped. It actually won a world award for its landscaping..

New Zealand breweries owned probably half the hotels in New Zealand, which surprisingly enough amounted to probably 200 or 300 hotels of varying sizes, because they controlled the liquor and beer in these hotels and that was the mainstay of the industry. So many managers were vying for the job to open up at the newest and nicest hotel in New Zealand, except me. I really was not interested because Warner's was more my style of hotel and I really enjoyed the publicity that I had been getting in managing this very fine hotel. But sure enough New Zealand breweries offered me the job to open up the new Russley Hotel. And so once again, I was on the move to another hotel. But it had its advantages. It had a beautiful manager's apartment with its own garden and this was nice considering my son Warren was now almost one year old.

The hotel also had some other interesting amenities that only if you had been to New Zealand and understood the business could you really comprehend. For instance, we had what is commonly called in most parts of the world, a bottle store where you served bottled spirits and draft beer. Well this one particular bottle store employed 22 people and behind the bottle store were huge stainless steel vats that each held 54 hogs heads, a hogs head being approximately 63 gallons, so one tank held about 3,400 gallons of beer. The hotel had 10 tanks, or half a million 10 oz. glasses. I have never seen so much beer consumed in one place in all my life. We would have such parking problems on a Friday and Saturday that you simply couldn't park within a mile of the hotel. We had one bar called the Garden Bar that was 5,000 square feet and you had to queue up for self service with trays that looked a little bit like the old fashioned container that you used to poach eggs in. In other words, a tray with six holes in it where you put glasses and then walked up to the counter, had them filled, paid, and sat down in the Garden Bar. We were also taking in huge amounts of money. It's the only new hotel that I've ever managed in my life that in the first year of operation made enormous profits.

We were also the place to hold functions and one or two amusing incidents came out of running some rather rowdy functions. One such function was for the local nurses, 300 of them, with their escorts, who all proceeded to get slowly smashed throughout the evening. Finally, 300 nurses in ball gowns all started jumping in the swimming pool at midnight. On another occasion, we had the local Chamber of Commerce who brought in a Fijian Fire Walker and Fire Eater. In the middle of the Ballroom they set up a temporary metal tank full of coals, someone lit the coals some hours before the function and then during the course of the evening the Fijian Fire Walkers would walk over the coals much to the amusement of the 400 or 500 attendees. That was really not the problem. The problem came when he started to eat fire and spit the flames out. I was sitting in the front row and suddenly realized, before I could stop him that he was going to hit one of the sprinklers. Sure enough, off went the fire alarm and down came the water drenching everyone in the ballroom. At least they put the fire out in the middle of the ballroom rather quickly.

Another absolutely crazy incident in the life of an hotelier also happened in this hotel. We had installed in the guest rooms new fiberglass toilet seats and over a period of two or three days the

Mr. T's team in 1965 at the Russley Hotel
in Christchurch, New Zealand.

housekeeper was finding in many of the rooms that the toilet seats were split and shredding for no apparent reason. Well, the mystery was solved when we discovered that staying in the house were 15 or 20 Japanese golfers who were playing on the championship golf course next door. When returning to the hotel and not being used to western toilets, they were standing in their golf shoes on the top of the toilet seat. How one of them didn't break his neck, I will never know.

I guess the crowning glory was meeting and having the Beatles stay at the Hotel, one evening I took them to the bar and bought them a beer and John Lennon explained to me he had come up with the name of the Beatles from the French Les Beat, little did I know that they would become so famous I would be seeing them in the future quite a few times.

I was still doing my radio broadcasts and writing the newspaper columns, and was an advisor to the New Zealand meat producer's board, and another member of the board was Graham Kerr.

I had also been invited to make a proposal to do a television show, and found out Graham was also doing a show. He had a great personality and was a great showman. At the same time both he and I had been asked to think about possibly making a trip around the world to promote New Zealand lamb and New Zealand produce such as kiwi berries, passion fruit, tree tomatoes and other exotic fruits that were grown and produced in New Zealand. Well, Graham Kerr got the television program and as many people know went on to make millions all around the world with his famous television program "The Galloping Gourmet." I, on the other hand, did the world tour which probably did more for my future career than anything else I had done so far.

CHAPTER EIGHTEEN

Trade Mission

The chairman of the New Zealand meat producer's board called and asked me if I would accept an assignment to lead a trade mission to promote New Zealand lamb. I accepted, of course. The trip was an incredible opportunity to see Canada and the United States at the New Zealand government's expense. I was to visit Vancouver including the island of Victoria, Edmonton, Toronto, Ottawa and Montreal. I was then to travel to the United States, visiting New York, San Francisco, Los Angeles, and return via Hong Kong.

It turned out to be a lot of fun on one hand; but on the other hand, a grueling trip with every step of the way orchestrated by a professional public relations company. Obviously it was to expose New Zealand lamb and other products and, as it turned out, we got plenty of that.

I had written a cookbook, published by a company in New Zealand called Whitcombe and Tombs, and several other promotional pieces with unique recipes using New Zealand lamb. These were to be used as part of the promotion. Of course working for New Zealand breweries, I had to ask their permission. They thought it was a great contribution to the New Zealand economy and said that I should go. In fact, they gave me some spending money and hoped that I could also promote New Zealand beers along the way. If nothing else, this was going to give a lot of exposure to the hotels that I was managing.

The New Zealand meat producer's board had done things in style. I was traveling first class. They had allowed me a two-day stop over in Hawaii. And when I finally arrived in Vancouver, I was met by my PR chaperone. Along with him was an Australian character by the name of Henry Welsh. Henry was an expert meat man; he worked in Chicago as a consultant in the meat markets and was an expert on everything from growing the beef to butchering it. Henry and I would be partners in prime.

The next morning we flew to the island of Victoria in a small sea plane and arrived at one the most incredible hotels I had ever seen. The Empress of Victoria was an unbelievable edifice situated in the middle of lawns and rose gardens right on the harbor of Victoria. I was told that in the early days this was the stop over on the Canadian Pacific luxury liners, and everyone stayed at this hotel. I asked the PR gentleman to see if he could arrange a tour of the hotel since it looked to be something very special and he did.

Actually, it was a little disappointing. It was much more impressive from the outside. I was told that it was built by an eccentric architect who indeed did build it from the outside and then went in and designed the interiors. I understand that he killed himself before it was finished - another budget overrun. The inside of the hotel was really rather tired. It reflected the fact that it was run by a railway company, the Canadian Pacific Railway. Like the railway hotels in London, they seemed to have a different atmosphere. However, at one time it had been a grand old lady and little did I know that some months later I was to return to this hotel and return it to its former glory.

The next morning the fun started. We were to demonstrate recipes using New Zealand lamb at a local TV station network. We had understood that local suppliers were going to deliver the lamb to the TV station where there was a demonstration kitchen. Wrong! Luckily enough, we arrived an hour early to familiarize ourselves with the kitchen and found there was no kitchen and there was no lamb. We immediately went into a panic. Rushing around, we bought a chafing dish with a Sterno heater, some oil, and the only lamb we could find was a frozen leg of lamb. We then had to buy an extremely sharp knife. We arrived back in the studio with a basket full of groceries and some ideas of what we were going to do. We took the leg of lamb, carved paper thin slices off the leg, dipped it in egg and crushed peanuts, and fried it in hot oil suggesting that this was a new Japanese way of cooking with lamb. The dish was an instant success and the station got many phone calls and requests for recipes of which we had none. I suggested to the PR representative that in the future he check on the supplies and said that I hoped this was not a forerunner of what was to come.

Back to Vancouver and on a new TV program, this time they had a kitchen. We had an interesting time with the local personality and some local chefs, indeed cooked up some interesting dishes.

The same evening we left by train from Vancouver to go to Edmonton. I had not realized that we were going to travel through the Canadian Rockies. We got up early at five o'clock in the morning just as we were entering the Rockies and enjoyed an unbelievable trip through Banff and Lake Louise, arriving the following midmorning in Edmonton where we were to go on another local TV program.

The day was uneventful except that when we arrived in Edmonton, it was announced by the conductor that it was 32 below. Well, having lived in Australia or New Zealand for the last almost 10 years, I really didn't know what 32 below was. I didn't even know what it was below. Let me tell you, it was cold.

In Edmonton we did the same series of TV demonstrations. In addition, we prepared a great dinner for the local food and beverage society and continued on to do the same thing in Toronto and Niagara Falls. It wasn't until we got to Ottawa that anything out of the ordinary happened. There we were the guests of the New Zealand high commissioner, an interesting man who wore a patch over one eye and looked more like an elegant Prussian spy than a diplomat. He lived in a magnificent mansion and had a Phantom V Rolls Royce limousine that he sent to our hotel to pick us up. Things were looking up.

The commissioner had arranged a dinner party for some 200 guests including some notable Canadian politicians. He had put at my disposal a catering company, pounds of fresh New Zealand white bait, fresh trout and salmon, fresh baby legs and racks of lamb and cases of wine. All I had to do was make the menu, supply the recipes and supervise the crew. Well, according to the newspapers, it turned out as one of the finest dinners ever put on in Ottawa. It was so much the social event of the year that it generated an article in the local newspapers on my various exploits managing hotels in India, refurbishing hotels in Hong Kong, and managing hotels in New Zealand, as well as, according to the reporter, being an accomplished chef. Great publicity and as a matter of interest it stimulated a phone call from Patrick Fitt, president of Canadian/Pacific Hotels, since he had learned that I was to visit Montreal the next day, that's where the home offices of his company were. He asked if we could meet, I replied, "Delighted."

"Lunch," he said, "at the Beaver Club, 12:30?"

"Sounds very Canadian. See you then."

The Beaver Club was indeed a great Canadian tradition. A wonderful, old restaurant that looked more like a gentleman's club, full of business men, and interestingly enough it was situated in the Queen Elizabeth Hotel which I learned was operated by Canadian

National the competition to Canadian Pacific. Patrick Fitt explained over a two hour, two cocktail, and one bottle of wine lunch that he was looking for someone with an unusual background, someone who had experience in operations and also had refurbished hotels, someone he could use to interface with the present management that will soon be retiring and a team of designers, architects, etc. Would this be something that I would be interested in? "You haven't told me what hotel it is," I said. "I am sorry," he replied, "It's the Empress Hotel in Victoria, British Columbia." "I know it well," I replied. "You do?" he asked, rather surprised. "Yes," I said, " it's very tired. The main dining room needs some special touch, the woodwork is magnificent, but it needs cleaning and that burgundy ceiling needs lightening up. The lobby bar is totally out of date. The last time it was refurbished it wasn't done well. The lobby needs something to give it action. It's too vast and empty." He was absolutely flabbergasted. "How do you know all this?" he asked. "Well you see, I have a great interest in the great hotels of the world and make a point of studying them and of course the Empress Hotel fits into that category and by the way you have a very talented chef in Mr. Bryan Thompson." He sat looking quite nonplussed. Of course I didn't have the heart to tell him that I had never heard of his hotel before last Monday. I got the job starting six weeks from the day of our meeting.

The rest of the tour was a blur in more ways than one because our schedules were so hectic. Henry and I had taken to having a couple of Manhattans before going on the air to sort of perk us up. Well, in New York, we were to go on the program of a famous local chef of some repute, James Beard and demonstrate how to bone, prepare and cook a leg of lamb. An easy assignment and Mr. James Beard had a wonderful kitchen in which to demonstrate it. The only problem was that fifteen minutes before we were to go on the air, we found out that the leg of lamb was frozen solid! Well, I had explained that Henry was an expert meat man, an would demonstrate how to bone a leg of lamb, so we decided that what he should do was carefully with a very sharp knife bone the leg of lamb while it was frozen, put it all back together again, and then when we were on the air, we would just fake it. Henry duly boned the leg and I very carefully put it back together again, put it on a silver platter and decorated it with little parsley, etc. It was a thirty minute program. I made the introductions, "Good evening ladies and gentlemen, Henry Welsh an expert artist butcher is going to show you how to bone a leg of lamb, something very few know how to do, and it needs a special talent." At which point Henry took his knife, waved it in the air, you recall we had already had two Manhattans, slashed the knife backwards and forwards like something out of an Errol Flynn movie and held up a bone that was completely bare of any meat, time 35 seconds! Twenty-nine and a half minutes left to go on the program. The live audience was so amazed they gave him a standing ovation. No one had ever seen anyone perform an operation like that in such a short time. Henry looked at me and grinned and said "Over to you." For the next 29 and a half minutes I had to talk and put on the show of my life. Actually I gave some interesting ways to cook lamb. In any case, it was a success and James Beard congratulated us both on a great program.

I returned to New Zealand via London meeting with some food and nutritionists and some other people to promote the lamb and then onto India doing the same thing and finally stopping off in Tokyo, Japan and going on a Japanese program which was probably one of my more embarrassing times on television. I was to demonstrate with a local lady chef the art of preparing lamb. The New Zealand meat producer's board was trying to introduce the taste into schools for school lunches etc. so that they could at least introduce to the Japanese the taste of lamb since most Japanese had only tasted mutton during the war and didn't like the flavor or the smell.

The demonstration went well however the lady chef had me sit down at a table and taste a few interesting Japanese specialties. One of which was a bulb of seaweed which she proceeded to offer me between chopsticks as the camera closed in for a tight shot. As I put it into my mouth and bit into it, the most putrid taste I have ever experienced exploded in my mouth and I must have looked as if someone was trying to poison me. I never did see the video to see what my face looked like.

Finally arriving back in New Zealand I told my wife and my young son that I had been offered a fabulous position as General Manager of a sensational hotel so we were off to Canada. Everyone thought I was crazy just to pick up and move so quickly. I had really established myself as one of the top general managers in New Zealand, but I felt that New Zealand was such a small country and that although I was doing well, my prospects were limited. I thought Canada and then perhaps the United States would offer a more rewarding future.

CHAPTER NINETEEN

The Empress Of Canada

The Empress Hotel was considered one of the grand old dames of the world. The hotel was built in 1908 and consisted of 160 rooms. It is rumored that the architect built the hotel from the outside and then designed the rooms and public spaces to fit and in many cases they didn't. He also supposedly committed suicide before it was completed, not that I understand from budget overruns, but a fateful love affair. Over the years, more rooms were added and finally in 1929, the hotel was completed with 572 rooms, an impressive property.

The foyer and the public rooms are faithful reproductions of English manor architecture so much so that in the 30's men would remove their hats on entering the hotel. Of course when I visited the hotel in the late 80's tourists wore shorts and T-shirts, so much for tradition. The hotel had six spectacular suites, the vice regal, the

Jacobean, one with a Spanish Italian flavor, and three other also very opulent as well as over 40,000 square feet of ballrooms and ancillary spaces. The hotel, however, still looked like a railway hotel inside with very little finish or gingerbread as we call it. The hallways were very plain. The hotel really didn't live up to expectations. You expected to find elegance and apart from the lobby and the ballroom, the rest of hotel was quite disappointing.

The general manager was I think worn out. He was due to retire and the staff knew it. The first thing I did was put together a renovation team. I interviewed architects from both New York, Toronto and Vancouver and selected finally a local architectural company headed by a very talented gentleman named Reno Negrin.

I then went to New York to meet David Williams a well known interior designer who had come highly recommended and was directing the renovation of the Chateau Chaplain for Canadian Pacific in Montreal. I also went on to interview other designers in Toronto and Chicago, but finally decided on a local Vancouver company simply because it was much easier to deal with architects and designers that were close to home rather than long distance in New York. It was also cheaper because you didn't have to pay the fares or for that matter the exorbitant fees. The company that I selected was a company named Hopping Kovach and Grinnell. They were all very individual characters. Art Hopping was the managing partner of the company and a very good designer. Kovach whose first name was Rudy was an artist and a temperamental one at that but a great renderer with great taste.

The first thing we needed to do was make an impression to attract attention so we started in the lobby, gold leafing painting , something that would attract the attention of the media and bring in an audience. The next thing was in fact to create an audience and we reintroduced high-tea in the lobby. It had always been there but it had deteriorated into tea and a few sandwiches in one corner. I suggested that we bring

The Empress Hotel in Victoria, Canada.

back tea trolleys and have an extraordinary variety of teas, wonderful pastries and scones and we imported Cornish clotted cream. It took off way beyond our expectations and the media picked it up. So popular was the idea that we decided to call the whole four million project "Operation Tea Cup" and the locals loved it.

The renovation of the rooms was really not very complicated. It was a matter of bringing them into the twentieth century with new but traditional furniture, modern telephones and all the amenities the guests looked for. But there were some interesting twists and turns as I have previously explained. The building was in fact built from the outside and it is hard to believe, but that there was a series of rooms where the windows were five feet off the floor and unless you were very tall you couldn't see out of them. Quite bizarre. They were also quite small in size. So we decided to combine these rooms with another to form a suite. In the first one we made a rather spectacular honeymoon suite, where the bed was raised off the floor on a platform and then on top of that we had put a very high four poster bed so they could see the wonderful harbor, and then used the sunken area for the living area. It was really rather gorgeous and very different and made great use of the room and its disabilities.

We had just finished the honeymoon suite and we were admiring it when we bumped into the chief executive of British Columbia along with his entourage and he asked to see the suite. So along with him, his entourage and some of our staff, some 15 people, entered the honeymoon suite. We were all standing around admiring the room and the furnishings when there was a scratching at the door and a key was inserted in the lock. Silence fell over the crowd. All of a sudden the door was flung open and a young man appeared carrying a bride across the threshold and much to his amazement a reception committee of more than 15 people including the Prime Minister awaited them. I don't know who was more surprised, but the prime Minister introduced himself, congratulated the couple and everyone filed out after shaking hands.

We had also refurbished the vice regal suite which was full of incredible antique furnishings, wonderful paneling and very little had to be done to bring it up to what really was its full opulence. The bathrooms had to be modernized and some furnishings had to be added to soften up the suite but it really was magnificent and again in order to get some publicity and some write ups in the paper a visiting actress Jayne Mansfield was invited to stay in the suite. Jayne Mansfield was to say the least a flamboyant woman. She arrived with a small poodle dog that was given a lot of attention.

I had personally shown her to the suite, pointed out the wonderful accoutrements and along with a reporter and a photographer had some photographs taken for the local papers. While I was showing her around the suite, she asked me if I would be kind enough to show her the wonderful building that she could see from her room which was in fact the House of Parliament. I said of course I'd be delighted and that afternoon with her dog and a photographer in tow. We crossed to the impressive parliament house which was not in session and we were duly given a tour of the building.

There was in this magnificent hall the seat of power where the prime minister sat during the proceeding and unfortunately Jayne Mansfield thought this was rather funny and proceeded to place her dog on the ornate chair. This immediately caught the attention of the photographer and the reporter and a photograph was duly taken. Unfortunately it was not well received by either the locals or the prime minister and I am not sure whether we got the right publicity. The caption under the photo was something like, A Tale of Two Sitters. But we certainly got the publicity.

Refurbishing and renovating the guest rooms and public spaces such as the ballroom were really a matter of good taste in maintaining traditions of the hotel. The restaurant on the other hand was a different matter. Something dramatic had to be done and someone needed to retrain the employees, design new menus and kick some life into the whole food and beverage operation. Presently, it was ruled over by a maitre d' who was a wonderful old Italian and who had been with the hotel for 50 years. He knew service and he knew how to treat the customers, but he was too old and what we needed was a food and beverage manager, someone who understood that each facility had to be a profit center.

In the steward's department which is the department that basically orders all the food and general supplies for the hotel was a young Englishman by the name of John Williams, newly married and new to Victoria. We immediately became friends and understood each other and he understood my goals and was very keen to help. I requested that he join our team and direct the opening of what was to be two restaurants. Canadian Pacific agreed and he was a great addition.

In the lower lobby was an old-fashioned coffee shop. It looked like a railway cafeteria. We designed a bright and interesting room which we called the Garden Café, not terribly original, but we took some ideas from the very popular Brasserie, of the same name, in New York. I could not understand with all the magnificent gardens around the hotel why this room couldn't be entered from the outside and why it couldn't look out over the gardens. I asked the contractor and the architect if we could not add a door in one of the walls facing the garden. They explained to me that this was almost an impossibility because the walls of this hotel were almost three feet thick but that they would look into it. I suggested that it was really appropriate that a particular location should be tried to be opened up. It was absolutely incredible. The contractor broke away the plaster in order to determine how thick the walls were and found to everyone's amazement huge double doors were hidden behind the plaster. Obviously, at one time the entrance had existed. In fact, once they had cleaned away all the plaster and masonry, the doors with a little oil literally opened and on the other side they had been bricked up. So, ta-da, we have our entrance to the gardens. Another interesting thing was that after we designed the room, I felt there should be more lighting and suggested we install wall sconces in certain locations marked with a felt pen. The electrician came back to me and asked if I would be concerned if we were to move the positions of the wall sconces a few inches higher and I said no, why? He said because that's where they were originally and all the wiring is still there, so I guess there's nothing new in this world. We just keep on reinventing what was originally there.

In any case, we opened up the room with lots of greenery, wrought iron, nice doors to the outside, and it very soon became a very busy restaurant.

On the lobby floor was the main dining room, a truly magnificent room with hand carved wooden beams, paneling and wonderful paintings, but it was so old fashioned and so forbidding that no one ever came into the room except to see the almost mediaeval architecture. We decided that we would make it into a more interesting restaurant with different levels and a dance floor and perhaps even introduce a show on Friday and Saturday nights, something that had not existed in Victoria at that time. My architects came up with a very interesting floor plan with several multiple levels and indeed a dance floor and a little stage for some entertainment. They introduced some interesting colors that gave sex appeal to the room and we finally had ourselves an interesting space. The next thing was to find some entertainment. John and I decided to go down to Seattle which is where most of the West Coast entertainment agencies were and visit with them to find out the type of entertainment that would be appropriate for staid Victoria. We found a real character by the name of Bill Burnham, an agent who handled a number of acts that seemed very suitable for the room, including the original Ink Spots so he took us out, plastered us with cocktails, and we agreed to run two or three of his acts. Later that evening both John and I were pretty much under the weather but we decided that we had to go out to a restaurant and we had been told that the best restaurant in Seattle was the Dublin House and that it in fact was very similar to the concept that we were planning.

We arrived at the Dublin House, a very charming Irish restaurant, very pleasant. However, by that time we were a little bit drunk, but we sat at the table and were given the menus. I said to John that it may be a waste of money because the menu was sort of floating in front of me to which he waved his hand saying, don't worry, and then promptly knocked over the oil lamp in the middle of the table which unfortunately spilled the oil onto the tablecloth which in turn caught fire. I looked at this rather rapidly developing situation and decided to remedy the situation. I turned around, picked up the ice bucket from the next table, graciously removing the bottle of wine, and tipped the content on the table. Needless to say, I put out the fire, but also destroyed the tablecloth and the table and the ambiance, at which point John Williams turned to me and said, "Well I really didn't like the look of the menu anyway so let's leave". We guiltily left, leaving chaos and destruction behind.

Despite this disaster we did book some great talent including the Ink Spots who maintained they were the originals. Not knowing too much about the history of American entertainers I was not in a position to disbelieve them. In any case they were a great success and performed for many weeks to a full house.

Working with Parkinson was not easy. He disagreed with just about everything we wanted to do and although I had the authority of the president of Canadian Pacific it was a battle each time. The only saving grace was his secretary Norma, a pretty plump lady around 25 who looked like a librarian wearing her hair in a bun and wearing horn rimmed glasses. She was, however, a great liaison and kept the peace.

Obviously, as I came to the end of the first year of the project it started to slow down. We had renovated just about all of the rooms, opened up new restaurants and I was looking forward to taking over the general manager's position. In fact, I had gone to a lot of trouble designing a special manager's suite on the top floor overlooking the harbor just so that my wife and I would be comfortable. The project had been a great success to the point that it had stimulated an article in Time magazine referring to me as an international hotel expert so I was positioning myself correctly, and building a nice resumé.

I received a phone call from an Alan Baker, president of a Canadian catering and vending company based in Toronto. Had I heard of them, No sorry I replied I hadn't. He explained his company was owned by a large American food service company and they had a very exciting project that they thought I would be tailor made for and they wished to talk to me about it. If I would meet with them Mr. Baker would send his Lear jet for me in Vancouver.

First of all I wasn't even sure where Toronto was. I looked it up in the map and it looked quite a long way away, but I decided that I had nothing to lose, so would certainly go and listen to their proposal. The following day I took a ferry over to Vancouver, went to the airport and sure enough there was a private Lear jet with two pilots and I was duly flown to Toronto.

I was surprised at the rather long journey but it was an exciting flight in a private jet, complete with a bar and a rather well prepared buffet lunch served by one of the pilots. On arrival in Toronto, I was met by an impressive Cadillac limousine with a chauffeur called James and I was taken to the headquarters of Versafoods. It was now 5:30 or 6 in the evening. Alan Baker was a very impressive distinguished gray haired gentleman in his early 50's.

He was extremely friendly, and offered me a drink and proceeded to discuss a possible future over a bottle of Singleton malt scotch out of Baccarat crystal glasses. A nice start I thought. He explained to me that his company had been bought out by an American company and he had made several million dollars in the transaction, but in the process had agreed to start a prestigious restaurant company for his American counterparts and that my job should I choose to accept would be to form a company and put together the most elegant and prestigious restaurants ever assembled in the USA under one roof. Well, he talked a good story and we polished off a bottle of scotch at which point he asked me if I would like to join him and his wife at his restaurant in the city on the top of the Toronto Dominion Center. It was called the 54th and naturally was on the 54th floor of the building. He was very proud of the restaurant and in fact it was a very elegant restaurant run by an Englishman by the name of Jimmy Hooks.

On the way to the restaurant, we had picked up Baker's wife and the three of us had a rather pleasant if not slightly inebriated dinner and by the end of the evening I had agreed to take the job and to start some four weeks later which I felt was not bad timing since the Empress project was coming to an end, a shame because what I really wanted to do was to be the general manager of the Empress, however this new venture seemed much too good to turn down.

The next day coming down slightly to earth I returned to Victoria on a normal flight, on a normal airline told my wife that we were moving to Toronto and started to compose a letter to Patrick Fitt.

Talk about perfect timing. I received a phone call from the general manager of the Royal York Hotel in Toronto who was staying in the hotel and he asked if I would meet with him. The Royal York was the largest hotel in the Canadian Pacific chain and their flag ship, the GM was making a bid to take over the job as president of Canadian Pacific thus ousting Patrick Fitt. I met with him and he told me that if I played ball with him, he would appoint me as the regional director of the west coast of Canada. In return, I had to agree to support him by suggesting that Patrick Fitt was incompetent and out of date in his thinking.

Evidently, Patrick Fitt had opened the Chateau Champlain, a hotel in Montreal that was way over budget and the company was looking for a scapegoat and this gentleman was obviously taking advantage of the situation, a typical corporate ploy.

I explained to him that number one Patrick Fitt had employed me. He had been an excellent employer and because of that my loyalty was with him. Under no circumstances could I say anything detrimental about Pat Fitt. He explained to me that Patrick Fitt was near retirement anyway and what did it matter and he went on to explain that he had been with the company for quite some time and he was next in line anyway and it was just a matter of time

First of all I didn't particularly like the man and secondly I was now thinking that it was obviously better for me to look to the future in Toronto since these inter company politics never worked out and someone would obviously move in after this gentleman and on and on and on.

So I played the loyalty a little bit to the hilt and finally said to him that quite frankly I would rather resign my position and that in fact I would do so and notify Patrick Fitt in the morning, explaining to him your offer and the fact I want nothing to do with this style of company politics. This didn't make him at all happy. Who said that I had to make him happy?

One month later, I did leave rather sad to see the back of the Empress Hotel. It was a great magnificent old dowager but as it turned out I did the right thing. This gentleman didn't last in his position and over the next couple of years I followed the progress of Canadian Pacific and there were numerous changes.

CHAPTER TWENTY

From Vending To Luxury

My arrival in Toronto was a little confusing. Baker's secretary had made arrangements for us to stay at a local hotel, The Seaway, close to their offices and right on Toronto harbor. They had also arranged for a rental car, so I was very comfortable. However, upon arriving on the first day to meet with Alan Baker, I was told that he was in Europe for a week. No one else knew of the arrangements he and I had made so I had to simply wait his arrival. I walked around the City of Toronto and became acquainted with my new surroundings.

Sure enough, Alan Baker arrived back on the weekend and apologized for the confusion and asked to meet with him on Sunday at which time he explained he was leaving for the Caribbean the next day to look at a future project. He also announced that he had made arrangements for me to go down to Philadelphia and meet with the

Chairman of his parent company ARA, and a few of the executives and talk with them about their future plans. He said that they had a plan to acquire some of the best restaurants in the US and gave me a list to research. Things were moving a little too fast for my liking.

Not knowing too much about American restaurants at the time, I did not realize that I had a list of the top 10 restaurants in America, if not the world, starting with Ernie's in San Francisco and ending up with the 21 Club in New York

So on the following Monday, leaving my wife and family in Toronto, I flew down to Philadelphia to meet with Bill Fishman, the President of the company. He insisted on being called Bill, which was very strange for me to call the boss by his first name. Bill was a very pleasant man, who obviously controlled an enormous empire. He endorsed the view of Alan Baker that we should pick up these fine restaurants and that I should make a tour of the various cities and inspect the books to see what I thought they could be acquired for and all the necessary travel arrangements were made for me to leave that afternoon.

For the next two weeks, I traveled to San Francisco, Los Angeles, Chicago, and New York, talking to some of the most interesting people in the restaurant business. I probably learned more in two weeks about some of the finest restaurants in America than most have learned in a lifetime. They were very interesting and very experienced owners who, for the most part, said that the restaurants were for sale but were very reluctant to open the books which were in each case two sets - one for the IRS and one for the operators. Each simply wanted offers to be made to them, rather than disclosing any figures.

After careful thought, I had decided that to put together such an eclectic group of restaurants such as these under one corporation was really not very practical. As far as I could see, a corporation such as the one that either Baker or Fishman ran was not the type that could run a group of family-owned restaurants, however while in Chicago

I had seen the amazing new 100 story Hancock tower, and had a wild thought.

On arriving back in Toronto and meeting with Alan Baker, I expressed my doubts to him. But, I also suggested that since he was so proud of his restaurants on the top of the 54-story Toronto Dominion Center, that if his American counterpart wanted to make an impression, they should lease the top floors of tallest buildings in the world starting with the Hancock tower in Chicago and build restaurants on them. This would certainly be an interesting innovation and should get ARA the type of publicity and image they were looking for.

He was very excited by this thought and suggested that we fly to Philadelphia to talk to Bill. We got him on the phone and within half an hour we were off in Baker's private jet to Philadelphia. He certainly didn't waste any time and apparently neither did anybody else. Bill thought the idea was great and said we should immediately investigate the John Hancock Building in Chicago.

Baker and I flew back to Toronto and he suggested that I immediately begin by finding out information about the various tall buildings that were being built around the country. Two days later, I had identified the Hancock Building in Chicago, the Bank of Indiana in Indianapolis, and the Bank of America in San Francisco, and they were all interested in a roof top restaurant.

Baker agreed that these were great buildings and said that I should immediately fly down to Philadelphia to discuss them with Bill.

Upon arriving in Philadelphia, I was met by a character by the name of Joseph Vannucci and I don't know who was more surprised, me seeing this blue eyed Sicilian in a dark suit and a red convertible or him seeing this crazy Englishman in a tweed suit and suede shoes, stepping out of a Lear jet. Many times after we became good friends and discussed this first impression. We both thought the same thing, "Who or what the hell is that!" and had a good laugh.

Bill Fishman thought the concept was a great idea and thought that I should set up my offices in New York at Kennedy International Airport at the home office of Air La Carte which was a division of ARA's. I returned to Toronto and told Baker the plans. He wasn't too happy about that but said that if that's what Fishman wants, I should immediately go to New York. So I went back to the hotel and told my wife that we were once again moving,

We had acquired my wife's brother's son, whom we were looking after while the father went through a divorce and of course our son Warren, so it was a little more complicated but Janice was excited about going to New York.

For the next two weeks trying to work in New York, find an apartment and find two children a school was simply a disaster. I did not know my way around and people were suggesting that I take an apartment in a complex what seemed to be hundreds of people in 4 or 5 high rise apartment buildings which was totally contrary to my previous way of living and I simply decided that I couldn't live in New York. I suggested to Bill Fishman and to Baker that since I was going to be traveling across the country that I should set up my offices in Toronto. Thank goodness they both agreed.

In the meantime, with the help of ARA lawyers, we had been successfully negotiating for the top floors in various buildings and I was now working with an interesting character out of the Philadelphia office of ARA named Ivor Christenson and it appeared that we were going to invest somewhere in the vicinity of $15 to $20 million. We also had to establish a team of interior designers and kitchen planners, etc., so I started to look for a suite of offices in Toronto where we could set up various designers, draftsmen, etc. I found a set of single floor offices in Rexdale just outside of Toronto. All seemed to be falling nicely into place.

Alan Baker called me to ask me to go down to see him in his office. When I arrived he suggested that I interview a woman who was an interior designer that he thought would be excellent for the overall project coordination. She was a French countess by the name of Anita De Vienne and it was absolutely my decision whether to engage her or not but that he would appreciate it if I would interview her. She evidently was a friend of his. I said I was pleased to oblige and he said that he would have his plane pick her up in Montreal and bring her into Toronto the next day. Well, Anita turned out to be a gorgeous blonde of around 36 years old. A French Canadian, she was previously married to a French Count. She was extremely vivacious and from what I could learn, very talented as a designer. As the conversation went along a precarious decision had to be made, but I decided that she was much too gorgeous to turn down. After checking her previous jobs, one of which was the Italian Pavilion at expo 67, I decided she was a talented designer and would be great to have around.

We had a pleasant lunch and she informed me she was off to New York to visit with some friends. I decided that I should get to know her a little better away from Toronto so I explained that it was a great coincidence that I too was flying to New York that evening and would she like to have dinner. Much to my surprise, she agreed and sure enough that evening, we met in New York and had a crazy evening on the town. I realized that I was treading on very dangerous ground. However, we took a handsome carriage to a restaurant, got drunk and had a wonderful evening. Somewhere around one o'clock in the morning, she impressed the hell out of me by drinking a yard of ale, which is one of those tall glasses that holds 64 ounces that they used to hand up to the drivers of the pony express in the old days.

The next day, I returned to Toronto and found out that the Chicago project was very close to a deal and proceeded to set up the offices. Anita would join us one month later. I also proceeded to hire a project manager, a couple of architects and some kitchen designers. It seemed as if we were in business in a big way and along with the momentum we were creating some publicity.

The Financial Post, a prominent newspaper came out in Canada with a large article about my company capturing some of the largest design contracts for restaurants in the United States. Of course, it didn't point out that we were working for our parent company and gave all the credit to the little company that we had called Planned Food Facilities International Limited.

ARA was a fascinating company. Its principals were interesting characters. Evidently, they were gentlemen who individually owned vending companies in major cities across the United States including New York, Los Angeles, Chicago and the Midwest and amalgamated into one company sometime in the late 50's.

I say the Midwest because when I met one of the principals over an elegant dinner in the Keys restaurant in Indianapolis, where we were planning a location, I asked him what his base of business was and he replied that he certainly was in the vending machine business but that he really made his money running the largest string of whore houses in the Midwest. I am not sure if he was pulling my leg, however as we visited a couple of night clubs that evening, it was evident that everybody knew him, particularly the girls.

It was agreed that the top of the 100-story John Hancock building in Chicago would be the first great location for a restaurant so I gathered all the information on the building and along with Ivan Christianson and a couple of lawyers we went to Chicago and started final negotiations for the space. Two months later, we had leased not only the top two floors, but 20,000 square feet on the lower levels, making a total of 60,000 square feet, which was pretty mind-boggling for developing a group of restaurants. I don't think there was anything of that size in the country, possibly in the world and I must say it was very exciting.

We hired architects and with Anita's help, a group of top designers and the project began. No sooner had we started on the drawings, than we were on our way to San Francisco to negotiate the space on the top of the Bank of America building and shortly thereafter the top floors of the Bank of Indiana in Indianapolis.

Anita and I were coming up with various concepts for restaurants and then flying to these locations on a weekly basis working with the architects and designers so that we could really introduce some new innovations into the restaurant field.

The first dubious experience I had in Chicago was with the building department. We had produced some preliminary drawings and decided that we should probably talk to the building department together with the health department to make sure that we were proceeding with their blessing. I made an appointment to meet with a gentleman who was one of the Building Commissioners and with a rolled up set of preliminary plans I set off to meet him at his office. He was an overweight slob and asked me where I came from, suggesting that I had a strange accent. When I explained that I came from England, he said, "What the hell are you doing building restaurants in Chicago and what the hell would you know about our codes?" I proceeded to explain that we had hired a very competent group of architects, in fact the company that had designed the John Hancock Tower and that we would call upon all the expertise necessary to see that we were going to install the finest of facilities. He told me that I hadn't got a hope in hell of proceeding and that they were so overloaded they couldn't possibly give us the permits that we were looking for, unless of course, I was prepared to pay cash for overtime that was needed to expedite the preliminary drawings. I explained to him that I was a country boy from England and that this was all new to me and if he wouldn't mind I would make a fast phone call to my boss and check it out with him. He agreed that that was a good idea and he suggested that I think in terms of $10,000 or $15,000 dollars, which was a large sum of money in those days in anybody's language. I called the President of the company in Philadelphia, got him on the line and told him my predicament. He asked me the gentleman's name. As it happens he had a name plaque on his desk. I proceeded to spell the gentleman's name into the telephone. I was then told to sit still in the office, make pleasant conversation and he would rectify the problem. The Building commissioner asked me why I was spelling the name out, "Well I don't know, maybe he was writing a check." He said, "I do not want checks, I just want cash because I have to pay all these guys under the table and it couldn't go through the city's books, otherwise there would be hell to pay that he was giving me priority, and I said not to worry, I am sure that it could be taken care of. Sure enough, five minutes later after talking about the weather, the phone rings and the building commissioner listens quietly on the telephone for two minutes. His rather boozy red face turning a shade of pale gray. He then proceeded to hang up and asked me for my plans. Without even looking at them, he stamped them, got out a book, wrote a certificate, told me to go to the other various departments and we were in business. So much for business in Chicago. We never experienced another problem in Chicago from that day to the opening of the restaurant.

However, one day I was sitting in my office in Toronto with Anita looking over the plans and we were expecting a visit from Bill Fishman and Alan Baker. Together we were going to review the plans and make sure that everybody was in agreement and that the project was going in the right direction.

Fishman arrived before Baker and we proceeded to open a bottle of Scotch and sit around and talk about the restaurant. Fishman suddenly realized that the traffic was going in the wrong direction around the John Hancock Building and this was not very good for the restaurant. I explained to him that there was nothing much we could do, that was the way the building was designed and what suggestion did he have. He suggested that I go down to Chicago and resolve the problem by getting the streets changed. I said I really didn't think that was very possible and he said, "Mr. T., as I was to be called in the future, I can assure you in Chicago, anything is possible." You go to

Chicago tomorrow and I will see you get to the right people. A few phone calls later, I had an appointment with City Hall in Chicago

The next day I flew off to Chicago and not only had a meeting with some official from City Hall, but was ushered into the inner sanctum of Mayor Daley and three of his subordinates. What ensued for the next 45 minutes was out of comic opera. I started to simply state that it was the wishes of Mr. Fishman that some consideration be given to changing the direction of the traffic, but before I could even get out a word, I was screamed at by Mayor Daley, saying that I had come here to try to push around the city and the language and the obscenities were unbelievable. I kept on simply stating, may I explain why I am here, to which I was met with a shouting barrage saying, "They knew why I was there, and that if I thought I was going to get away with that, whatever that is, I was mistaken." Obviously, there was either a good relationship between the company and Chicago or a bad one and I never really found out, except that the traffic patterns were eventually changed.

A few days later, I was out to San Francisco with an appointment to meet the President of the Bank of America, Rudy Peterson, at the Bohemian Club. Traveling along with me was a principal of Cushman and Wakefield out of New York, the company responsible for the leasing of the restaurant space and retail spaces for both the John Hancock and the Bank of America buildings. His claim to fame was that he left school at the age of 13, had survived in the city of New York and was now a multimillionaire. He was the most likable, if obnoxious character you could ever meet, his language was incredible. Every other word was an obscenity, but he was very interesting and we got along well on our flight to San Francisco. On arrival, we first had a meeting with the bank to put forward our schemes for the restaurants and to also present a suggestion that we build a banker's club with, obviously, no amount of money being spared. During the course of the meeting, other business was discussed including a point that evidently there were some new bids to be put out for some steel work. I only bring this up because the president of the Bank of America suggested that it was not necessary to put it out for bid, that it would be much quicker for him to discuss it with a personal friend of his and one of the customers of the Bank of America who he knew would give him the best possible price, at which point, the gentleman on my left from Cushman and Wakefield turned to him and said, "You're a fucking idiot. I'll never know how you made it to the President of the Bank and that anyone who would give out a contract of that value without a bid should be put to sleep." I can't elaborate but it went on for about 15 or 20 seconds and you have to remember that the president of the bank was a gentleman and a very sophisticated one at that and I have never heard anybody addressed in such a manner. Obviously, Cushman and Wakefield were doing a great job because Peterson simply brushed the comments aside and said that he would discuss it with his executives. But over the months, this character from New York abused everyone, never stopped shouting and screaming and I understand several years later, he died choking on a piece of steak in a restaurant. I am not surprised.

Working in San Francisco was also an experience. We were working with a design company that supplied most of the furniture fixtures and equipment for Hotels in Las Vegas and were supplying the kitchen equipment and preparing some working drawings for our restaurants at the Bank of America. They had acres of display showrooms and were very efficient. However over two or three dinners with some of their principals we realized they were running a dubious organization. At one dinner it was suggested that I purchase a few shares of their stock, which was currently trading at around $42 and that I should mortgage everything that I own to buy the stock. On the other hand I should not try to contact them for the next 10 days because everybody was going to be out of town on business.

I did not have the money to go out and buy the stock, which was most unfortunate, for in the next week, it went up to $160. Then it was suspended, a judge who was on their board was charged with accepting bribes and the company was charged with fixing a football team and the whole thing collapsed in some sort of scandal. This didn't seem to interrupt their business abilities and they continued to complete our drawings and supply the necessary equipment.

On one occasion, I was driven to Las Vegas to look at a couple of large hotel kitchens that this company was installing along with some proposed restaurant design work. We drove down in an Aston Martin at 100 to 120 mph all the way. Upon arrival, we were treated like royalty. One evening, I was taken on a tour of the casinos and shown the catwalks above the gambling tables where they scrutinize the gamblers and croupiers. I was also privileged to be shown the silver truck leaving Las Vegas, which was the truck that collected silver from the various casinos and changed it into paper while doing a circuit around the countryside. It was interesting because it was not only armored, but several guys rode shotgun. It was obviously their way of skimming from casinos, I was told that they exchanged silver for notes at a number of Churches. True or not, I would never know.

We also saw great shows and I was introduced to Frank Sinatra at Caesar's Palace, as he was doing a show there at the time. Everybody seemed to know everybody else and it seemed to be literally one big family.

The other extreme was dealing with the Bank of Indiana. A more conservative group of people you couldn't find. The president of the bank's name was Weatherspoon. It gives you an idea of the people we were dealing with. From one extreme to the other. In the meantime, we had also acquired a project in New York to build the restaurants at the BOAC Terminal at Kennedy International Airport and this took a number of flights from New York to London and back, negotiating with the various architects that the British wanted to use. This job was outrageous and one of the most ludicrous projects that I have ever had to deal with in my life. Dealing with the contractors and the unions at Kennedy Airport was a nightmare and the project was costing twice as much as anything else we were doing in the United States,

BOAC called a meeting on the airport site to express their dissatisfaction at the incredible rising costs and the lack of cooperation. The gentleman that they sent to chair the meeting was out of Gentleman's Quarterly wearing a three-piece suit and a gold watch on a chain, a bowler hat and carrying an umbrella. He was what the British called a Quantity Surveyor.

I, too, was in a three-piece suit and certainly looked English but somehow I managed to have a relationship with the contractors even though I thought they were crooks and stealing us blind.

BOAC was not wrong. For instance, the construction hadn't even begun and BOAC wanted to change the drawings to make it easier to operate, and already the contractor was charging extra for altering the project and where anything else could be built in the country for $60 a square foot, this was not in excess of $200 per square foot, so the quantity surveyor from London started to make his speech and I must say it was a little bit out of a comic opera with him sitting at the end of the table talking to about 25 or 30 union construction people who thought he was something that had flown in from a Mary Poppins movie. After about 15 minutes, the project boss who was sitting next to me, kept on saying to me, "What is he talking about, what is he saying? What language is he speaking?" And it was true, they were totally on a different plain. After about 10 minutes, the job supervisor asked me if I would go outside and talk to him for a couple of minutes, which I did, and he politely suggested that I tell this crazy Englishman to go back home and leave them to do the job or he would end up in the Hudson River with concrete boots on. Unfortunately, he was serious. I went back in and asked the quantity surveyor to step outside and expressed the same sentiments. He couldn't believe it and he said, you're living in some sort of fantasy land, those things are only spoken about in cheap dime novels and I intend to see that this job is brought in on budget. However, I did suggest to him that maybe we could compromise and have some discussions with contractors and report back to him, which we did and we did get some minor modifications and cost reduction, but the small mobile office that the quantity surveyor had set up on the sight to work from disappeared during the evening with all their records and was never found again and I think he got the message that they were serious and left for London. When the job was finally finished, it was almost twice what the original budget was and it wasn't even that good.

New York, Chicago, Indianapolis and San Francisco all going full speed ahead. In the meantime, we had taken on a hotel at Toronto airport to be called Heritage Inn and had acquired an in-flight catering company in Jamaica that had the rights to all the airline feeding in and out of Jamaica and were drawing and designing the commissaries in Montego Bay and Kingston.

I was traveling around in a Lear Jet accompanied most of the time by Anita and project managers and kitchen consultants that we had on staff. Our weekly circuit was New York, Chicago, Indianapolis, San Francisco, Toronto, Jamaica, London and on and on and on. Everything was going smoothly until my project engineer in Los Angeles quit because he said with three children and a family he didn't want to be mixed up with the people that he was dealing with out there, which was a little puzzling, because in all the dealing I had with them, although they obviously were a bunch of gangsters, they were polite to me, put no pressure on us to buy anything that we didn't have to buy and did everything on time and well.

Working in Jamaica was another kettle of fish. Trying to plan buildings and get them built with local politicians and labor was a slow and arduous task. We were also doing a lot of high finance. Most of these projects were management contracts and the owners such as the Bank of America were spending their money and not that of ARA'S. However, in some instances, ARA was also putting up money, as in Jamaica.

Traveling with us was a young comptroller by the name of Jim, who had totally gone berserk with the idea of the Lear Jet and the chauffeur, and the hotels and the glamorous life and was starting to drink and go a little crazy. He happened to be an amusing fellow and played a couple of tricks on me that at the time were funny. One, for instance, when we were staying at the Sheraton in Kingston, he had picked up a six-foot, rather gorgeous black Jamaican girl at the bar, paid her the going rate, got my key from the front desk, had taken her to my room, got her undressed and then left taking her clothes with him, leaving her naked in my room. When I arrived back at 12:30 in the morning, I found this six-foot raving naked maniac in my room doing a rain dance or something similar. I explained to her there was nothing we could do. I couldn't get him on the telephone and I had no idea where her clothes were. I suggested we just make ourselves comfortable and we could see what could be done in the morning because I had to be up early for breakfast. I simply checked out at seven leaving her there to her own devices.

It was a wild town in those days and we all used to end up at a nightclub called the Big Bamboo, where we used to drink too much and the local native girls got up on the tables and did strip acts and they weren't even paid to do it. One night we got back to the hotel with Jim, who was drunk out of his mind, got him to his room, where there was a small narrow balcony with a much too low railing all around it. Unfortunately, Jim walked out onto the balcony and thought that he was in the hotel that he had been in three nights before in Germany, where there was a terrace. He flipped over the rail and fell four floors down to the swimming pool deck, broke his collarbone, legs and arms and was out of action for six months. I guess the great life had got to him.

We had so many projects going in different parts of the world that we were forever traveling. It was a wonderful time for Anita and I but unfortunately not much of a life for my wife back home.

However, life was not too much fun anymore. We were working six and seven days a week, traveling enormous distances and times and in a lot of cases, taking advantage of the time change, going out to the west coast and back. We were two years into the project, the restaurants were ready to open and they were quite sensational, but I was getting to be simply a puppet of ARA's.

We had taken on a project in Los Angeles and I was getting very little satisfaction out of seeing anything mature, because we were simply running around putting out fires all over the country and trying to keep all the projects in line and to me, life is just too short to work that hard with very little satisfaction, and while I used to think that ARA wouldn't go to the washroom without checking with me first. I felt that, by the same token, if I had a heart attack I would simply be pushed aside and that would be it, not that I was contemplating a heart attack, but I was working enormous hours and very, very hard. Also, Alan Baker was getting upset with me in Canada because I was spending more time with his mistress than he was, his mistress being Anita of course. So one Sunday arriving back from the west coast at 4:00 in the morning, I decided that was it. It was not the business that I really wanted to be in, it was fabulous money, but there was more to life than that. So, I decided to bail out and return to the hotel business, which was really my first love. On the other hand, I had gained enormous experience in the restaurant field, which would be invaluable to me in future years. As it turns out, the restaurants were all very successful. ARA didn't hold onto them all because one of their senior officers, Ivor Christianson, who also worked with me on the projects, left and started his own company, and took away a couple of the locations. But they certainly all exist today and they are all busy.

Life suddenly changed for me. Anita left with me, and I decided to get a divorce and make plans to marry Anita.

We were married at a friend's home, John and Doe Serentino, who had a Sicilian style estate with the most magnificent setting on the lake, just outside Montreal. They invited 120 friends and guests and put on a most unbelievable banquet.

CHAPTER TWENTY ONE

The Proverbial Consultant

I think that every hotelier sometime in his life decides to be a consultant. Unfortunately, it's usually when they are out of a job and when they can't find anything else. But I had made a lot of contacts and decided to set up shop in a small suite of offices in downtown Toronto. At least if I was not successful, it would give me breathing time to look around for another good job.

Evidently, my contacts were working. The phones starting ringing and I received several calls. One was to take over the management of a hotel in Niagara Falls, New York called the Red Coach Inn owned by a gentleman by the name of Bruno Scraffri. I agreed to go down and take a look at the property and meet with him. It turned out to be a charming old English inn on the edge of the American Horseshoe Falls It needed some minor decorations which Anita could take care of and some intensive management. We negotiated a management fee and I was to take over the following Monday morning.

I called John Williams who was still in Vancouver and he was delighted to come to Toronto and join me. He needed a break from what he was doing at the Empress.

The next call was from another Italian gentleman who had through his company purchased a city block in downtown Toronto on which stood a four story tavern which only served beer and was also very busy. He needed management until they could come up with the plans to develop the property. I agreed to go down and have a look at the tavern and again we negotiated a fee and took over the operation of the tavern. This turned out to be quite an experience. First of all, all the staff looked like body builders. I was later to find out they were all ex-cons, however they successfully carried three trays of stacked beer glasses up three flights of stairs.

The interesting part is that it really was quite a fun place and we developed three floors of entertainment. We hired an Irish singer by the name of Mo Magenty who played the guitar on one floor. A Hindu by the name of Cedric De Croix who played the piano and other entertainers who simply started to make this place the in place in Toronto even though it only served beer.

We were going to a number of social functions around Toronto making a number of friends and would turn up at eleven o'clock at night along with a crowd mostly in black tie. This made for a very interesting mix of customers since most of the others were in t-shirts and jeans but somehow it blended and everybody loved the different types of crowds to the point that everyone ended up singing and standing on the tables and chairs around one o'clock in the morning.

There were a couple of interesting incidents. One day one of the waiters came to me and told me that his grandmother had died and left him some stocks and bonds and that they really didn't know much about them and wondered if I would like to buy them or if someone else that I knew would like to buy them. He then proceeded to dump an envelope of bonds on my desk from all the major companies in Canada and the United States to the tune of around $350,000! 1 asked him if I could keep them a while and look through them and he said by all means. I made a couple of phone calls and decided that they were obviously stolen and that I really shouldn't have anything to do with them and I didn't.

Later I found out that a customer who used to come continually into the tavern became involved in the bonds and also got shot at from a car parked nearby and thus confirming my suspicions that they were stolen.

On another evening, John Williams who was managing the tavern approached me in the tavern with some friends when he came to see me that he had a problem and wondered what we should do about it. There were three rather large black gentlemen who were selling marijuana on the staircase and they were not about to move because John Williams suggested that they should. I accompanied him in my black tuxedo and confronted the gentlemen and said that if they didn't move we would have them thrown out to which they suggested that who was going to throw them out? At that point, about three tons of waiters appeared around the staircase and the gentlemen obviously got the message that they could in fact be thrown out without any trouble. At least our staff was loyal.

I don't know why but all my contacts seem to be Italian. I got another call from a gentleman who said that he had a restaurant north of the 401 that my management would not interfere with that of the owners of the present establishment since his family operated in a different area of Toronto. I was starting to believe that I had made contacts in some dubious circles however I went up with Anita to look at his restaurant and again we took it over to straighten out the management and make the place a little more interesting. Later, during our discussions with this gentleman we suggested that he should not invest too much in his restaurant since there was a new restaurant opening up only two blocks away and it appeared that they were going to go after the same clients. He was obviously a little upset by this discovery and said that he would look into it, but continue to develop his restaurant and bar.

A week later the new restaurant had an unfortunate fire and never did get off the ground.

I then got a call from a gentleman who owned a building in Lewiston, Niagara Falls. It was a fabulous landmark called the Frontier House, an old inn. The question was would we be interested in creating a restaurant and bar and running it for them? John Williams and I ventured down to Lewistown and decided that it was a wonderful old building with great historic value and two weeks later we took over and came up with an idea for a great restaurant and bar.

We were making a reasonable living but I really missed the operations of hotels and I got a call from a friend who told me that the Parker House in Boston was looking for a general manager and they thought that I may be an ideal candidate. I told John Williams that I would go down for the interview and if I got the job there was no reason why he could not continue to run our small operation in Toronto, I may be able to feed him some possible clients from the United States.

We had in fact been operating these various establishments for over a year. One of them turned out to be not very successful and that was the Frontier House and unfortunately we had signed an agreement whereby it was more of a lease than a management contract. So we decided to close the restaurant down which brought on a very funny incident.

Everyone agreed that the lease could be terminated, particularly since the owners had found a willing lessor in McDonalds and was going to turn the Frontier House into a McDonalds. That was a shame but probably a very good use for it. In turn, John Williams and I had to vacate the premise which was full of a fair amount of liquor which we had duly paid for but since we lived in Canada we weren't quite sure how we were going to get the liquor back into Canada, but we devised a plan. I had a rather large S-1 Bentley and we discovered that by removing the back seat we could stack quite a few bottles of liquor underneath and undetected drive them across the Rainbow Bridge into Canada, each time we did it we were asked if we had anything to declare, we replied no and we went through the border. However, this was to come to a rather funny ending. We had really got all the serious liquor out of the restaurant and were left with all the most unusual bottles of liqueurs - Ouzo, Galliano, Roman sambuca, anise and all the things that one normally never drinks. We decided in one last effort since we had had such an easy time going through the border just to put them all in the trunk of the car and chance it. Well, sure enough when we crossed the border they asked us if we had anything to declare I said no and they asked me to pull over to one side. A customs officer on opening up the trunk was mildly surprised. John Williams was casually smoking with his foot on the fender and I suggested that we had been to a party the night before and forgotten that we had the liquor in the trunk and we were just returning home.

Not believing us, the customs officers along with a couple of helpers unloaded the trunk of the car onto the counter in the customs offices. There must have been forty bottles none of which anyone could recognize as something you would normally drink. They asked us if we ever drank scotch or gin. We laughed and said we really liked exotic and unusual drinks.

To cut a long story short, they fined us five hundred dollars, confiscated all our liquor which I am sure they gave away for Christmas presents, and then when we were about to leave, they asked if I would like my car back. I said why wouldn't I want my car back? And they told me it had been impounded for smuggling. If I wanted it back, it was going to cost me another five hundred dollars. A rather expensive day.

We went back to the Frontier House the next day and decided that we had at least two cases of rather good wine and should we take the risk by going across the border again and I decided that at least if nothing should take another bridge. So we duly loaded the wine under the back seat of the Bentley as we had done successfully in the first two or three trips. I then drove across another bridge without any incident and reached the Canadian side successfully. However, we still had another load left back in the restaurant. So I left John Williams with three or four cases sitting on a bench on the Canadian side of the falls and returned to load the final two cases into the car.

On again crossing the bridge, I was stopped by a customs officer who suspiciously looking inside the car and asked if this was an S1 Bentley to which I replied it was. He opened the back door and I thought that obviously the word had gone out and I was certainly going to end up in jail. He looked around the car very carefully and said to me that his brother was thinking of buying one just like it and he loved the car and suggested that probably his brother would do well as buying this as an investment, closed the door and waved me on through.

On arriving on the Canadian side, I was met by a rather agitated John Williams who rushing to put the cases of liquor into the car pointed out that I had left him in front of a building marked Customs and Excise.

I talked to Anita about the Boston offer and we decided to drive down to Boston and listen to a proposal to manage the Parker House of Boston.

CHAPTER TWENTY TWO

The Parker House

The Parker House was one of the oldest Hotels in Boston, run by a well known family, The Dunfey's. It was quite a family, something like 8 brothers and two sisters. They wanted to open a new restaurant in the lower level of the hotel and had a concept called "The Last Hurrah. " The family was very political and evidently the name was a play on a famous or infamous past mayor of Boston, Mayor Curley, and they wanted to create an old fashioned Boston nostalgic style restaurant.

I was to be the General Manager and we would live in the hotel with my new family which was now Anita, her daughter Nathalie, and my son Warren. The salary was attractive, and the challenge of once again creating a restaurant was fun and an easy project, so I accepted.

I had purchased a Bentley S111 in Montreal, a magnificent automobile. It was a one owner car with only 4000 miles on the clock, so we loaded the family into the Bentley and headed for Boston.

Boston was a wonderful new experience, I immediately went to work on the Last Hurrah. The Dunfeys had access to old memorabilia, and with Anita's help and many trips to old antique shops, I very quickly put together a restaurant that looked as if it had been in the hotel for ever. We looked for a manager and interviewed a few good prospects, however one day a gentleman walked in to my office and he looked like something out of central castling. He looked about 50, he was short, his hair was parted in the middle, and he wore pince-nez, those little spectacles that Victorians used to perch on the end of there noses. He was from a past era and asked if we needed someone to play the piano in the main dining room. His qualifications were that he played the organ in a local church and he was, without doubt, gay.

I said to George, as was his name, "How would you like a job as a restaurant manager?" He nearly fell off his chair, he replied he knew nothing about restaurants or management, I said I will teach you, you start tomorrow, in actual fact we had a food and beverage manager, and others who could take care of the food costs, staffing, etc. What we needed was someone to be the host, an official greeter. George was hired even though the personnel manager thought I was nuts, as I think did everyone else. George was incredible. We put him in white tie and tails and he added a monocle and stood grandly at the bottom of the stairs welcoming everyone. It was like walking into a Victorian men's club. Customers loved him. He also fussed over the wait staff, made them clean tables quickly and pranced from table to table chatting with everyone, I swear local businessmen brought clients not for the food but to meet George, and yes the restaurant was a great success, due in no small part to our character host.

The hotel was a different matter, I have never seen so many family members who wanted to tell me how to run the hotel and one brother would ignore what the other brother had told me. It was a ridiculous situation. In there opinion it was an elegant hotel. In reality it really was not, and they would not let me run it my way. I told them I could make The Parker Houses "The" hotel in Boston, if not New England. They simply said it already was.

After just six months, I was ready to quit, which meant moving back to Canada, however we had a ski chalet in St. Adele, just outside Montreal. I was very disappointed. I had done a great job on the restaurant, but failed for the first time to make an impression on the hotel itself.

Just as I was going to give my notice, and make arrangements to move, I received an invitation to interview with the Sheraton Corporation, someone at the Parker House had a friend at Sheraton, and suggested they talk to me.

I met with Sheraton's corporate human resource director, after a two hour interview, the next day they offered me the position as Resident Manager of the Sheraton Boston, a thousand room hotel in the Back Bay area of Boston. I jumped at the opportunity.

CHAPTER TWENTY THREE

Sheraton Boston

They say that bullshit baffles brains. I had never managed anything like a 1000 room hotel, and I had no experience with corporate structures and budgets etc. It seemed they had had a large staff turnover and according to the general manager morale was down, and they thought my maturity would be a steadying influence. Actually I was only thirty six, but I guess with a beard, I looked wiser and older.

But from the word go, I guess I was not cut out to be a corporate employee, only the second week in the job, at a meeting with the regional manager, the corporate food and beverage manager, and a group of other home office types, a plan was discussed to renovate a small bar on the third floor of the hotel called the El Diable and to convert the room into the "Clip Joint", a bar modeled, don't ask me why, on a barbers shop, at a cost of $100,000. Evidently they had just built one at their hotel in New York, After reviewing some renderings done by a Chicago design company, most in the room agreed with the corporate F & B director, after all it was his idea, that it was a great concept. I was then asked what I thought, I replied it was the worst Jewish Miami looking concept I had ever seen, an awful idea. Not the kind of comment to make if you want to be a company man, and I added if they gave me ten percent of the budget I could do a better job.

Lets face it if anyone had experience with restaurants it was me, I think I was very unpopular but they said they would think about it.

Surprise, surprise, I was given the project. The outlet was really dilapidated and had been closed down, but with a very small budget, in just three weeks, with my genius designer Anita, the room was transformed into "The Upstairs Pub"

It looked like a real Irish Pub, already a good idea in Irish Boston, we had plastered the walls with stucco, inserted old looking faux Tudor style beams into the plastered walls, hung inexpensive factory style lights, put sawdust on the floor, placed bowls of peanuts in their shells to throw on the floor. Anita found peasant style blouses, to make the waitresses look like wenches, and the final product looked quite genuine for $10,000. Mind you we did all the work with in-house maintenance workers. 1 had brought my old entertainment buddies Mo MacGenty and Cedric De Croix from Toronto and in one month the room generated $180,000, a record for a bar in the Boston Sheraton. It went on to generate $600,000 in the next six months. Of course, they thought I was a work of genius! By all looks, I was going to do well with the company.

Even though I had not had the corporate training in budgets etc., I quickly caught on, and was initiated by fire. Within a month we were going to have a review of our next years budget. David Samedeni, the very experienced front office manager and I spent long hours into the night building a previous history of the Hotel's occupancy and room rates and to our dismay found out both occupancy and rate had declined for the last four years, also there was less future business on the books than the current year. David explained there were also two new hotels in the city, there was no alternative but to show little or no growth next year. Remember all this was done by hand-written documents, no computers. I was to present the budget along with a couple of department heads to the 12 member review team from the home office. After I made my hour and a half logical presentation, the regional director Hal de Ford said it was totally unacceptable, we must increase the occupancy by eight percent and room rate by a dollar twenty five, which would improve the bottom line by over a million dollars, end of discussion. I interjected that that was completely illogical and why would we do this in the face of the facts. First of all there was silence as every one thought about my next job, then Hal De Ford said because that's what ITT, the owners of Sheraton, expected and secondly because as he said " I said so." I said but when we don't make the budget, what about our credibility?

After a long silence, with a great deal of paper shuffling around the table, because no-one questioned Hal De Ford, he suddenly said, "Meeting over!"

I thought perhaps I should keep a low profile for a while, no such luck. The Hotel was full and it was the busiest month, October. In order to get maximum occupancy the hotel was frequently over-booked, and to-night was no exception, and when you are over-booked and have no more rooms for guests with reservations, you " walk" them to another hotel, sometimes even to the suburbs. Obviously you get some very irate guests.

I was relaxing in my apartment when I received a call from the front desk saying they had a serious problem. They had to walk a very unhappy black caucus because there were no rooms available and they wanted to see me in the lobby. I asked, "What the hell is a black caucus, some sort of monster?" Sir, you had better come down, was the answer. "It's Jessie Jackson!" I said OK I am on my way, but who is Jessie Jackson? I have heard of Jessie James.

It may have been better if it had been Jessie James, it would at least have been a quick death, because in the middle of the lobby was a black gentleman, at least he was a gentleman until he spoke, surrounded by six or eight of the biggest black men I had ever seen. I said good evening, and was immediately verbally bombarded with some very unsavory remarks and threats. They demanded rooms immediately or they would call the President of Sheraton, and sue the Hotel. I explained all the rooms were occupied and we had rooms for them at the midtown inn. They literally screamed at me and, after another round of abuse stormed out of the hotel.

Somewhat bewildered, I asked who or what was that. It was explained to me who Jessie Jackson was. "Oh well," I thought, "back to the suite, better start packing".

The next day I received a call from the President of Sheraton, who explained we had just made a huge blunder and that I was to find them complementary rooms immediately, I was to go to the Harvard Club, meet with Jessie Jackson, make my apologies, offer them free rooms and a cocktail party for their group, at the hotel's cost and that I should take Willie Armstrong with me. Willie was our black housekeeper, a terrific person. Why on earth would I take Willie I asked why not the front office manager. Because he is black and you will look as if you are not discriminating, I was to say the least dumbfounded, but if the President says jump, you say how high.

Off to the Harvard Club with Willie, I told him I was so embarrassed to involve him, and he smiled and said he understood, when we arrived they were already waiting with loaded guns. I apologized profusely, or though less and less enthusiastically, offered them the rooms etc. Jessie Jackson replied he would be the last nigger we would ever "walk" from our Hotel, I nearly fell over, and was mortified for Willie, I explained to them that when you made a reservation over the telephone, it is written on a form in quadruplet, the top was pink, the second green, the third blue, and the last white, none of the copies were black, so we did not know the color of our guests and walked out. My God, so much for keeping a low profile.

Could anything else go wrong? Of course the next week, the president of a company holding a convention in the Hotel, did not checkout of the Presidential Suite on the day he was scheduled to, deciding one more night, which he did not request from the front desk otherwise they would have told him the hotel was full and his suite already booked. Unfortunately another president of a convention was checking in and the Presidential suite was not available. In fact no room was available, period. He was livid. Finally we found a small studio room, and after plying him with Scotch, told him he would have his suite tomorrow, it would be complementary for the rest of his stay. Reluctantly, and in a foul mood, he went to bed,

That night a water tank broke on the 20th floor above his room and four thousand gallons of water poured out. I heard about this the next morning, I took the day off.

Managing this property was a great experience, initiation by fire so to speak.

One day, I got a call from a voice from the past, Lennie one of the boys from Toronto. A small group wanted to come to Boston to see the Bruins and the Toronto hockey team play, could I book them 5 rooms, and would Anita and I like to have dinner with them. I said of course, even two countries apart I did not want to offend them. Sure enough a week later they arrive, and in the hotel we had a dinner show The Fantastic, in one of the outlets, so I asked them if they would like to see the show, and they said sure. I think it was a bit tame for them, but we had a pleasant time, around 11 o'clock we broke up and they said they would get an early night, so we all parted in the lobby, they got into the elevator, and Anita and I prepared to retire also, however Dick Barger the GM was coming through the lobby having had a few drinks somewhere, so we talked for a few minutes. Suddenly out of the elevator comes the Toronto group all dressed to kill, shirts open to the chest, gold chains etc. ready to hit the town, they said Hi and were obviously a little bit embarrassed. Barger said who the hell are they, the local Mafia, I said no, just some friends from Toronto. The next morning Anita received 6 dozen roses.

Within three months fate again intervened. Sheraton decided to sell the Sheraton Plaza. A rather run down older property that they owned facing Copley Square, and next door to the 60 story Hancock Tower, was not doing well, losing a bundle of money.

They had first tried to sell it to Prudential who owned the Sheraton Boston, with the hope they would spend the money to renovate the Hotel and then give a management contract back to Sheraton. When that failed they approached the John Hancock Insurance Company.

John Hancock was having real problems with their new building, unfortunately the huge plate glass windows were falling out, a strange phenomenon, it was a wonder no one was killed since the windows were falling some fifty to sixty floors into the street.

Hancock decided to buy the hotel not because, as most people thought, to avoid potential lawsuits because of the windows falling out around the Hotel, or because of the alleged damage to the Hotel during construction, Hancock purchased the Sheraton Plaza, simply to protect the property in front of their tower.

In fact Hancock later asked me to prepare a law suit to sue them on behalf of the Hotel so that their insurance could pay for any serious damage to the Hotel, and in the end there really was very little.

Two Hancock executives, William Leary and John Worthen, from the realty division were negotiating with the Sheraton corporation and were the same people that I was involved with in building the restaurants on the top of the John Hancock Tower in Chicago.

The then chairman of Sheraton came to see me one day and asked if I would like to manage the Sheraton Plaza. He conveniently neglected to tell me that Hancock had requested that I do so, but simply took me on a tour of the hotel. I must admit I was not terribly impressed since the hotel was so run-down; it had been supposedly last re modeled in the late 60s. It had asbestos drop tile ceilings, etc. Sort of early depression, there were holes in the ballroom carpets and the most awful coffee shop called the Minute Chef.

At a meeting between Hancock and Sheraton, it was agreed that Sheraton was to retain the management contract on the sale of the hotel and I was to be the managing director. In front of both Sheraton and Hancock executives I said I would take the position on the condition they gave me at lest a million dollars to clean up the place. The Sheraton people were furious, first of all they nearly had a fit when I asked for a million dollars and they thought I would ruin their deal. Hancock was paying six million for the property, and I was asking for a million right off the bat, but since Hancock was calling the shots, everyone agreed. Interestingly enough even though Hancock agreed to fund a renovation, they told me later they themselves did not think the hotel could be brought back to life. I think they were thinking of pulling the building down and maybe make a park in front of their Tower. Little did they know their six million dollar investment would later bring a sale price of $56 million.

CHAPTER TWENTY FOUR

The Grand Dame

One month later, I moved into the Sheraton Plaza, with my wife Anita, her daughter Nathalie and my son Warren. We lived on the sixth floor which was the top floor, on the northeast corner overlooking Copley Square. We occupied a five-room suite, it was very spacious, but very tired, I thought if we could decorate our suite it could be like a show suite. Anita had the place painted by the in-house staff and stretched fabric on the walls, which was a little unique because she did this herself. We collected interesting pieces of furniture from around the hotel and, in a short time, with Anita's elegant taste, and some good shopping around the Antique stores, we added some very wonderful antique furnishings that we owned along with some great art, the result was a wonderful suite to entertain in.

In actuality over the years, the cost of us occupying the suite rather than renting it out to guests more than paid for itself with the publicity and guest relations. Anita and I entertained a mixture of local business personalities and many film stars, such as Yul Brynner,

Peter Falk, Van Johnston and at a one time Luciano Pavarotti who came to Anita's birthday party and sang *Happy Birthday* to Anita much to her surprise and that of our friends.

The first few weeks I just took inventory and found the 460 rooms were very tired. The restaurants consisted of The Minute Chef, labeled by the employees as Cockroach Alley, with good reason. Its clientele consisted at breakfast of the old drunks that came in for the ten cent cup of coffee, it was truly a greasy spoon. Downstairs was a restaurant called The Smorgasbord, which was in a function room and a leftover Idea from Dan Nyboe a previous Danish general manager, a very charming man, known as the Silver Fox. The Café Plaza was a tired but rather nice room that was only open for lunch and was a poor copy of the wonderful Oak Room in the Plaza, New York, and next door was the Merry Go Round, a bar that I would later find out was where most Bostonians were engaged or at least met there. It had a revolving bar in the middle, surrounded by some seats, upright poles and covered with a canopy. The whole idea was to make it look like a carousel.

An interesting little story that I was told and Dan Nyboe did confirm it was that Dan was a real ladies man, and one day he was riding around on the Merry Go Round flirting with two young ladies, at some point he put his hand up the dress of one of the ladies, and she quietly handcuffed his wrist to one of the Carousel support bars and poor Dan had to wait until the room emptied out so the hotel engineer could cut him loose.

Over the years the hotel was to become a consuming passion, taking it from a very tired old Sheraton Plaza to The Copley Plaza, and as *Harper's* and *Queen* once stated, "one of the finest hotels in the world." And, perhaps more importantly, from miserable losses to serious profits.

My office was situated on a sort of mezzanine floor it was a very unique office. With a large fireplace and a half-moon sunburst window looking out onto Dartmouth street,. The furnishings were very ornate and reflected the character of what I hoped would be the final look of the hotel. I sat behind a large Louis XIV desk and in front of me, two large Victorian armed chairs covered in a faded old velvet, all of which I found around the hotel.

Off my office was a glass bridge that spanned the lobby, but it went nowhere, I suppose it was simply an architectural detail since there was another at the other end of the lobby, however I later turned the one off my office into the resident managers office, that way he could see the whole lobby from the front desk to the other end of the lobby.

Sheraton had cut expenses to the bone, and had staffed the hotel with an eclectic but not very experienced group of department heads. Obviously I needed to build a team and hopefully I could train the present staff, if I was to reach my goals.

Each morning folding chairs were bought into my office for a daily staff meeting. My secretary a young Chinese woman called Norma, who was married to David Semadeni, the front office manager at the Sheraton Boston, took the minutes. Attending was the front reception manager, the chief comptroller, the banquet manager, the chief engineer, the food and beverage manager, the head housekeeper, the staff manager, more commonly known as the personnel director. After a couple of meetings I felt the most impact I was going to have to bring people back into the hotel was to create some interesting food outlets, so I asked Sheraton for a good resident manager to start to figure out where the losses were since I hated working with numbers and the business would better be served by my creating revenue centers and I needed an experienced food and beverage manager, since I had a lot of ideas.

Two weeks later Barger, the regional manager, said he was sending me two people who were considered good potential but according to other managers a little difficult to handle and maybe my maturity would be a good influence on them.

The first to arrive was Bill Heck, he came from a Sheraton hotel in Philadelphia where he was presently the resident manager. He was six-foot-four, twenty-three years old, and what I would call a typical American whiz kid, someone who had been trained in the Sheraton system, who knew numbers and could punch a calculator. He was perfect. The other a few day's later was Jean-Claude Mathot, a 250 pound, six-foot, food and beverage man, a Belgian who looked like he knew food and indeed over the years proved that he did. He had been trained at the CIA no not the intelligence agency the Culinary Institute of America. Little did Sheraton know that I would be more difficult than these two put together and both turned out to be part of my successful team for many years to come.

Once these two had familiarized themselves with the layout of the hotel, we had our first serious staff meeting, "Well, the first item on the agenda ladies and gentlemen is housekeeping. The hotel is dirty." "That will change," said Ms. Rebecca, our newly hired, tough outspoken British-styled housekeeper. "I start training classes today." A few days latter I saw her leading a six foot black houseman down the corridor by the ear to show him he had not done a good job on something, she was later to get me headlines in Newsweek and around the world.

"The next item is room's revenue. The occupancy at 63% isn't bad, but the average rate is a disaster." "Two problems," said the front office manager, "the rooms are tired and we have 120 airline rooms a night at $18 to $25 average rate. They are diluting the daily average rate and killing us. On the other hand, they generate some serious income".

I responded that in two weeks time, we start a complete renovation of the guest rooms, floor by floor. As the rooms go back in order we will not allow any airline crews in the new rooms and we will slowly phase them out. In one year we should have them all out of the hotel.

"Next on the agenda we have to do something unique with food and beverage."

Jean-Claude and I discussed the fact that we needed to create something that would attract attention and get us some publicity, I realized that in another two months it would be the 200th anniversary of the Boston Tea party, I suggested that we play on nostalgia and install a wonderful tea court in the lobby. The lobby was a vast empty space, so we thought we would create something unique. There was a small check room and I suggested Jean-Claude investigate installing a minimum pantry where we could boil water and make tea and coffee so we could offer an English style Tea, with scones and cucumber sandwiches. Here we go again, nothing is new.

Down in the basement were some old disused original 1912 employee wash rooms, now in storage. I discovered that the partitions between the toilets were black and white marble, some four feet by six feet and had them cut and polished and made into table tops. I also found in a salvage yard about twenty five feet of marble balustrade which we used to enclose the area. I purchased 40 Bentwood chairs and we had ourselves a Tea Court.

Two weeks later it opened for business and was an immediate success. I could not believe the interest. We had a press party opening and as was quoted in the Boston Globe "television lights shone over a group of tables each adorned with three-tiered epergne of hot buttered crumpets, triangle sandwiches of cucumber and tomatoes and of course scones and Cornish cream, the people seated were sipping cups of Darjeeling tea, white gloved waiters moved among them their expressions benign. "You've got class and elegance and that's what I like," a lady in a green velvet suit was telling an Edwardian looking gentlemen with a curled mustache. "I deplore the fact that class and elegance are nearly non-existent today." The Edwardian gentleman was none other than yours truly, Alan Tremain, General Manager of the Copley. The lady in the green suit was Hildegarde, the famous supper club chanteuse of the 30's, 40's and 50's, and playing Cole Porter in the background was another honored guest, the famous society band leader, Lester Lanin.

We got more than a full page in the Globe, by the famous columnist Bill Fripp, mention in the Herald American and the Christian Science Monitor, and even a spread in the Providence Journal. Every afternoon from then on, a small waiting line formed. I found George who had left the Parker House, and hired him as the Major domo. He was fantastic, dressed in tails he looked like someone from Alice in Wonderland strutting around warming the tea cups and chatting with the old ladies.

I always said, running a Hotel was like putting on a show, you created the scenery, your employees were the cast and the customers the audience. If they enjoyed the show, they came back.

Since it was December I also decided to put on a special bash for New Years Eve, which in fact was why both Hildegarde and Lester Lanin were at the opening of the Tea Court, they were to be the act for the Renaissance Ball.

Within two weeks we decided to knock out the walls of the checkroom and enlarge the pantry into a small kitchen, our clientele was everything from little old ladies with their grand children to Mary from Peter Paul and Mary. The Tea Court later on became a $500,000 a year profit center.

The Providence Journal Weekend put it perfectly. "May we direct your attention to what looks like the grandest New Years Eve party money can buy in this part of the country, the Renaissance Ball at the splendid old Copley Plaza." The funny thing was that the hotel was still officially called the Sheraton Plaza but people were already calling it as it was originally called.

The fixed price evening at $100 per couple begins with cocktails and sumptuous hors d'oeuvres including caviar at 9 o'clock, continuing with dancing to the famous Lester Lanin orchestra, whose next bash is the Inaugural Ball in Washington. At eleven o'clock you will begin a five course dinner, each course accompanied by a carefully selected wine.

Throughout the evening you may have your drinks refreshed. Hildegarde, the chanteuse will sing to you and when morning comes breakfast will be served.

I hired a local public relations company called Robert Wise & Associates to give us the entree into the local business community. Bob Wise was a valuable addition to our team and worked with us for more than 10 years, through some very difficult times, and always gave us the right advice.

An elegant invitation was designed and sent out to anyone who was anyone as they say, over 600 responded. A third were freebees given to corporate CEO's, however the actual cost of food, beverage, orchestra etc. was covered by those who did pay, and it was cheap advertising. The evening was a great success.

The ballroom was decorated circa early 1900's, with black and white center pieces, sort of Belle Epoch with long white candles. Jean-Claude and I designed an incredible menu duplicating and enhancing the inaugural dinner for the opening of the hotel in 1912. Starting with an egg that had been blown out, like you did as a kid if you collected bird's eggs, you made a small whole in the top and bottom and blew out the egg. Next we sliced off the top and filled the egg with scrambled eggs and caviar. Next course was a consommé, but with a difference. We gave everyone a tea bag in a cup on a saucer. The tea bag had inside a mixture of herbs and spices, the waiter then came around with a tea pot with a beef consommé, a uniquely different presentation. As a main course we had a fillet mignon of venison with a puree of chestnuts, and finally an individual soufflé. No one present could believe we could put 600 soufflés on the table, and actually Julia Child, who was attending with her husband as our guests, asked how it was done.

Anita and I had a table with the Chairman of Hancock and his wife, Barger and his wife from Sheraton, and Julia Child and Paul her husband, who I had become good friends with, we made a lot of friends that night. A new year had begun well.

It was time for new concepts. I had suggested to Dick Barger the regional manage that we needed to create a fun restaurant with access from the street. There was a series of very exhausted looking meeting rooms at the north east end of the lobby, but they had wonderful Adams style architectural details, I suggested maybe we should convert them into a great restaurant, there was direct access from both St James Street and Trinity Place, an absolute must for a new restaurant. He thought it wasn't a bad idea and would talk to Bill the VP of food and beverage for Sheraton Corporation.

The next thing I knew was Sheraton had solicited a proposal from a design company in Chicago. Unfortunately the same group that had recommended the Clip joint in the Sheraton Boston. I was invited to a meeting at the home office where they made a presentation to install a seafood restaurant. Renderings showed it like something out of Disney Land with a huge salad bar in an oversized rowing boat. The executives at Sheraton thought it was wonderful. I thought it was awful.

I got the ear of Hancock and proposed that we design a restaurant that was more in character with the hotel and suggested an atmosphere similar to a wonderful restaurant that had been around for a hundred years in London called Rules, an old Edwardian restaurant with walls covered with old pictures of famous actors and famous people of the time. A decor similar to this, I argued, would give the feeling of being part of the hotel, something that you would expect to find when it was first opened, in 1912. I had prepared a montage of photos from Rules and a very successful restaurant in New York called Maxwell's Plum. They loved it and told Sheraton that they would like to go with my ideas since they new my track record from Chicago. Sheraton wasn't happy, but agreed.

Work started immediately on what was to be called Copley's.

To help kick off the rebirth of the Copley Plaza, I had again suggested to Sheraton to drop the name Sheraton Plaza and rename the hotel "The Copley Plaza", and to remove the hideous neon sign on the roof. The Sheraton Marketing department went crazy. They said the sign could be seen for miles. I agreed, but said that was the problem. The Copley Plaza should not be lit up like Times Square. Once again I got the ear of Bill Leary, chairman of the realty division of Hancock. He agreed with me and told Sheraton he wanted the hotel to be called The Copley Plaza. The Bostonians loved the return to the original name.

I had found in New York a company that had all the old style metal shapes of Marques that dated back to the 1900's. I had them fabricate the original designs that had been on the Hotel when it was built in 1912, and made two new canopies over both the main entrances. I also had wonderful bronze plaques made with the back to back "P' the trade mark of both the Plaza in New York and the Copley Plaza, since both hotels were designed by the same architect.

There were two ornate lanterns on the Dartmouth street side of the building. I found an artist in Roxbury who could make this type of wonderful lamp, and for just $2500 a piece. I ordered 15 and put them all around the hotel which made an enormous statement. The old Dowager was really starting to put on the dog, as they say.

As we became more elegant, particularly in the Grand Lobby, we attracted the usual eccentrics that love to hang around hotel lobbies. One morning I had got up very early to go to New York, and arrived in the lobby at 5 a.m. The security man on seeing me said, am I glad to see you Mr. Tremain, there is an old lady that has been in one of the phone booths all night, and neither Jimmy the night bellman or I can persuade her to come out.

I went with them to investigate. We had a series of phone booths at the end of the lobby near Trinity Place, and as I arrived a little old lady came out of one of the booths. She wore a wonderful hat decorated with fruit, and was elegantly dressed, just like someone's grandmother, certainly not like a vagrant, I fell into step with her as we waked across the lobby, I inquired politely if I could help her. No answer. We kept on walking. Can I call someone for you, I suggested. Still no answer. Look, I said, let me get you a taxi, which I will be happy to pay for, to take you home or wherever you want to go. She turned to me and said, "Why don't you fuck off, sonny." Everyone died laughing, and of course it did the rounds of the hotel like wildfire.

We had placed 6 large throne-like carved chairs around the center of the lobby, and of course these became favorite spots to sit and watch the world pass by. A not unattractive young woman, perhaps in her late thirties, would sit in one of these chairs, particularly when we had a group in the ballroom, and she would make flirtatious eyes at the passing males, eventually some unsuspecting male would smile back and approach her and perhaps invite her for coffee in the tea court, much to his surprise and shock, she would at the top of her voice yell at him, "I'll give you a blow job, or go into the check room for a fuck. You're a pervert." Of course the lobby would grow silent and the poor unsuspecting male would get such a shock, would not know what on earth to do. Usually, he would skulk off, with the whole lobby watching him, and sometimes have to leave his conference in embarrassment. Of course these eccentrics were soon told to leave. Other lobby lizards would just fall asleep and snore, very loudly. I trained the bellmen to go and shake them awake and tell them an ambulance was on its way which made them make their exit immediately. In the end we had to remove the chairs from the lobby to stop these fruitcakes from bothering us.

One of the sad spaces in the hotel was the Café Plaza. At one time it was obviously an elegant room, when the hotel opened in 1912. This room was to the Copley Plaza what the Oak Room was to the Plaza in New York, after all both rooms were designed by the same architect and owned by the same company.

Whether there was a budget overrun or something else, the Café Plaza fell short of the Oak Room, the walls were half paneled and there was this coral-colored block up to the ceiling. The ceiling itself, however, was made of magnificent carved plaster.

In the sixties Sheraton had painted the walls a sickly pea green and put on the floor an awful nylon shag carpet. It only opened for lunch and when I arrived in 1972 it was a sad shadow of it's former self. Since the only place to have breakfast was the Minute Chef we opened the room for breakfast.

One Morning while Anita and I were having breakfast, I noticed the awful shag carpet was lifting in a corner of the Cafe Plaza, out of curiosity I pulled it up further to see what was underneath and to my amazement there was a marble floor underneath. I decided there and then as soon as the restaurant was closed for the day, I would explore further. I showed Anita, Bill and Jean-Claude and we all got so excited that that night, fortified with a few glasses of white wine and a huge pot of Jean-Claude Mathot's Moule Marnier which he cooked up himself in the kitchen, we moved all the tables and chairs out in to the lobby and tore up the carpet carrying it to the dumpster. Underneath was a fabulous floor of decorative marble. We worked until 3 a.m., sweeping the floor then replacing all the tables and chairs and reset the tables for breakfast. The change was incredible - the marble didn't even need polishing.

On one of our visits to New York to buy furniture for the guest rooms, we were rummaging around in an antique shop that specialized in ancient theater fixtures and found some old stage draperies that were so heavy you could not lift one panel, I said to Anita lets buy this and have them remade for the Cafe Plaza. The owner of the store recommended a very talented man who made draperies for the old mansions in Rhode Island and had, in fact, made the draperies for the mansion that was featured in the movie The Great Gatsby. We contacted him, brought him to Boston and showed him the old drapes.

He just beamed when he saw the material and agreed to remake the stage drapes into the most wonderful window drapes for the Café, They turned out to be quite extraordinary.

When you find such unique craftsman it attracts others and we were to discover another genius whose name was John Emmanuel. He was a Greek painter who could do the most amazing things with paint, faux marble or faux wood to such a degree that marble or wood specialists could not tell the difference. I explained that the oak paneling only went up about 6 feet, whereas in the Oak Room in the Plaza in New York had paneling up to the ceiling. I showed John pictures of the Plaza Oak Room. He said he could reproduce the effect, so we gave him the project. He did an unbelievable job in faux oak, painting the grain in with feathers, not only on the walls but on the ceiling beams that divided the ceiling up into two areas. He also antiqued the wonderful decorative ceilings.

The effect was so good that an old Boston dowager who claimed to have been coming to the Copley since she was a little child, remarked to me that she was so pleased to see us restoring the original wood paneling that she remembered from her childhood. I think the architect Henry Hardenbergh who designed both the Copley Plaza and the Plaza in New York, would have been proud of the finished effect.

Looking at some old original floor plans of the hotel that I found in the basement, I discovered that the Minute Chef, or Cockroach Haven, as it was called, occupied the original entrance to the cafe so I decided this should be reinstated as the main entrance, giving the room a direct entrance off the lobby. The result was a wonderfully intimate library bar seating about 25. It was beautifully paneled in dark oak, where the doors to the street were for the old Minute Chef, we had a fabulous stained glass window made that was actually two stories high covering my window in my office but from the street it really made a statement. The Library Bar soon became the hot spot after work for the local business types to have a drink and then it became a waiting area for dinner guests where they could have a drink and look at the menu order and when the chef was ready they could go to the table.

When the Café was finished with art on the walls, two crystal chandeliers from a Rockefeller estate in Rhode Island, good silverware and glass-ware, it was as good a restaurant setting as you would find anywhere.

As Jean-Claude was busy not only controlling expenses, but with me developing new ideas for the outlets, we needed some new talent especially a restaurant manager. We interviewed several people but one stood out whose name was Henry Ball. He had worked with restaurant associates in New York, and for the last year he was managing a restaurant in Cambridge that had a great reputation. It turned out Henry was a very talented restaurateur, but hard to handle. Most of the female staff complained he kept telling them he wanted to get into their knickers. Did I tell you he was English? Henry brought with him a young women chef, a first for us whose name was Lydia, and she was a very innovative chef, and started with Henry to develop some sensational menus.

Lydia was the chef of the Café Plaza for two years, and put the Café on the map as a truly four star restaurant, and she was ambitious, so much so that she wanted the job as chef of the hotel kitchens. I had a heated discussion with Lydia and told her she was fantastic in the Café but not running the main kitchen, which had about forty cooks. She got mad and so did I, I finally said " Lydia there is no fucking way you can run the main kitchen and you are simply not going to get head chef's Redmond's job"

She left sometime after that and went out to Los Angeles and then came back to Boston and started her own restaurant, which was an enormous success, we were still good friends, and one day with about eight friends I went to her restaurant for dinner, she made a great fuss of us, sending out numerous wonderful dishes, and at the end came out to say halloo to everyone, we applauded, she turned to me and said, " Mr. Tremain can I now run a fucking kitchen?"

After Lydia we hired a new chef who was also brilliant, his name was Jasper, we got rave reviews from food writers like Gus Saunders, and the Cafe was now a fully fledged elegant restaurant.

The maitre d'Hotel of the Café Plaza was Heinz a German who wore white tie and tails. He clicked his heels and almost saluted guests when they arrived. Heinz, at our request, was to make sure that all gentlemen wear a tie and jacket. It was, after all, a formal dining room. One evening a table of five arrived and one gentleman was without a jacket. Heinz requested that the gentleman put one on and was prepared to supply one. One of the group pulled Heinz aside and said, "Do you know who this gentleman is?" Heinz looked over his shoulder and replied, "Sorry no". At which point he was told that it was President Carter. Without missing a beat Heinz responded, "Then why doesn't he have a jacket?" Under the circumstances we did make an exception, but someone overheard the discussion and phoned it in to a local columnist, Harold Banks. We got headlines all over the country.

Zero Mostel was having lunch in the room one day and a group of ladies were having an argument as to whether it was really him. He obviously heard them because he turned around and sang, "When I was a rich man…" The ladies clapped and were very happy.

We were establishing the old Copley name with the Tea Court and now the Cafe Plaza, the hotel was starting to buzz. Refurbished rooms were coming on line and with them a more sophisticated clientele. However we were not attracting a young crowd, so I decided to follow up on my idea of the Rules of London type restaurant and bar.

At one end of the lobby were four tired function rooms called the State Suite, consisting of one large room and three smaller rooms.

They had very high ornate Adams style ceilings maybe twenty-five feet high. The corridors leading to the rooms were covered with black and white vinyl tiles under which we discovered the most sensational mosaic floor.

I decided to build a stand-up bar, the first ever in Boston, in the large room facing Copley Square. It would be modeled a little after Maxwell's Plum in New York. And the Restaurant would be situated in the series of small dining rooms off the bar. I called Ernie Fox in New York and asked him to come to Boston. Anita and I sat for two days and designed what would be a series of three Edwardian rooms each with its own unique décor. I had taken pictures of the famous Rules restaurant in London and wanted to cover the walls, as Rules did, with hundreds of pictures of famous people. Ernie was familiar with both Rules and Maxwell's Plum, and so he was able to interpret my thoughts exactly.

Obviously all the work had to be bid out, and each time in the past the successful bidder would be an Italian, by the name of Paul Perala. He with his band of carpenters was incredible. Most of the time we either followed Ernie Fox's renderings or drew the plan on the wall and built it. The painting was executed by our resident artist John Emmanuel who even devised a smoking technique to give the ceilings an antique patina.

We did the rounds of all the junk shops and antique stores, and collected a huge amount of pictures none of which cost more than a hundred dollars. A priest called me and said he had a huge, very erotic Bacchanalian-type painting that his mother had left him. He offered to sell it to us because he was too embarrassed to own it. We also bought a large painting called the White Rock Lady, a symbol for a soda pop company which became the subject of a funny story.

Some years later a story appeared in the Wall Street Journal that the soda company was looking for the original White Rock Lady painting, which depicted a naked nymph-like female on her knees looking pensively in to a pool of water. The paper said it was quite valuable, and the company wanted to find it. The paper went to quite some length to describe the painting and said because it was used as an advertisement the lady did not have nipples. Neither did ours, but we did not believe ours was the original.

I said to Bill, the resident manager, that we could have some fun with this and get some publicity, why don't we have it stolen? What gave me the idea was a strange event that we had recently experienced. A woman staying in the hotel had allegedly been robbed of $400,000 worth of jewelry. She claimed she had hidden it in her room then, when she found the jewelry missing, had called our security who in turn called the Boston police. She did not, however, want to make a big deal out of it because her German husband was on some sort of hit list. The next thing was we received a phone call from someone from the north end, an Italian voice who mentioned a reward and told the police he would only deal with me as a go between. Anyway, because it concerned a foreign national, the FBI took over. As this was still fresh in everyone's mind we decided to steal the painting ourselves and leave a ransom note on the wall.

We decided this was fun so agreed to meet in the restaurant at three o'clock in the morning and remove the painting to my apartment. We set our alarms and at the agreed time quietly slipped into Copley's only to find the night cleaners sitting in that room having a break. Ok, let's meet in an hour, at four am. We arrived only to find two security men having coffee. Shit, we thought and decided on 5 a.m. This time we were lucky, no one was there, but when we went to lift the painting off the wall we found it had been screwed to the wall. Later we learned that the chief engineer, Tom Banks, had read the article and, as a precaution, had secured the precious painting to the wall. So much for a life of crime.

Another talent came into my life. A starving artist named Ted Jacobs, from New York. I had found some old wall sconces in an old Schraffts restaurant that was going out of business. We mounted them on six foot mirrors around the bar and Ted painted nude figures holding them. We constructed a new entrance like an Edwardian Conservatory off of Copley Square. Ted painted the glass panels with wisteria. John Emmanuel did a Faux Bois ceiling and walls and we covered the canopy with ivy. The whole concept was stunning, it's only potential problem was everyone was telling me women would never stand around a bar in Boston. My, were they ever wrong. Copley's, our new restaurant as it was called was opened in April 1973 and was an instant success. Within six months it was reportedly the highest revenue provider per seat in the country, mostly from liquor sales. Even back in 1973, it would take in $8000 a night from the bar and that was quite something.

Marion Christie, a Boston Globe syndicated columnist wrote an article saying, "The swingingest singles bar in town is Copley's where the bankers and the investment group get together with the Gucci hip swingers." And indeed they did, it was wall-to-wall people at the bar.

As another public relations project I engaged Sebastian Cabot, who appeared in "Mr. French and Family Affair" on TV and played Dr. Wyatt in the TV series *Check Mate*. He was to be the official greeter standing at the door. People were so surprised and thought he was great. We became instant friends. So much so that he was only meant to be there for the two opening nights, Monday and Tuesday, which were special cocktail parties for the local business community. He decided to extend his stay at no expense. He said he liked the place so much and was having so much fun. Actually we did have a lot of fun, because when we opened to the public the look on people's faces when they came in was so funny. One day we took him to Durgan Park, a famous old restaurant in Quincy market, a place where you sit at a communal table. He loved it and when the dessert came, a strawberry shortcake which was majestically huge, which was their style, he remarked to

191

the waitress only a pig could eat that much, to which she replied, "You should be right at home!" It was a sort of trade mark for the waitresses to insult the customers. He loved it.

After a week of having him eat us out of house and home and drink us dry, I finally had to reluctantly drive him to the airport in my Bentley to get rid of him before he turned me and some of my staff into alcoholics. He was, to say the least, a marvelous character and a dear friend.

After just one year Copley's was generating more revenue from the Bar with its 120 seats than the rest of the hotel together.

This brought its own problems. One night someone broke into the bar and was in the process of stealing several cases of wine from out of the cellar when our security personnel caught him and called the police. The police commissioner, Bob De Grazzia, was a friend of mine and said if my security officers do their job properly then please follow up and prosecute, which we did. This meant our employees had to sit in court for several hours, only to have the judge dismiss the case. Very frustrating. A week later the same man returned trying to do the same thing. Again we prosecuted, again it was thrown out.

Would you believe he came back again and tried to take two large bronze lamps. This time we took matters into our own hands. Jean-Claude and I along with Chris the sales director took the thief and threw him into the huge trash compactor, then turned it on. He screamed bloody murder as it started to compress him. Of course we had no intention of following through. But when he came out he left in a hurry and never came back.

Another problem we had was that someone was selling drugs in Copley's kitchen. We decided to set up a hidden camera and find out who the culprit was. We had a professional set it up with the police commissioner. We caught one of the cooks not only selling drugs but he had a gun in a bag.

I didn't want any adverse publicity so, after talking to Bob, decided to have an employee meeting. The next day we called a meeting in the restaurant at 11 o'clock and I explained to all eighty employees that we had tape recordings of transactions taking place in the buying and selling of drugs.

I explained we had no desire to prosecute anyone and that the personnel director would accept anyone's resignation in the next half hour with no questions asked and nothing would appear on anyone's records. After the meeting ended Bill came to see me and said we may have a problem opening Copley's for lunch - eighteen employees had quit.

The public spaces in the hotel were now jammed. At one end you had Copley's which was bringing in all the young investment bankers and their secretaries and on the other end you had the Boston Brahmans. In between, the Tea Court brought in the grand mamas and their grandchildren. The hotel now was grabbing its own headlines, including "The Revival of a Grand Hotel," which appeared in a two-page article in the *Christian Science Monitor*.

Sheraton, for some reason or another, resented the success that I was having. They thought I was a loose cannon. Its' true that we were not conforming to the normal measuring yardsticks of the Sheraton corporation. On the other hand, John Hancock was thrilled with what was happening to the hotel. Bill Leary, the chairman of the board of the realty division, had stated that he thought the hotel never could be brought to its former glory simply because it was not the fashion to stay in the older tradition; it was more the fashion to stay in the new and modern properties, but now thought we were doing the impossible.

Bill Leary, said to me, "Look, I don't think Sheraton is doing anything for us for the fees we are paying, which are substantial and there is a clause which allows us to cancel the contract. How would you like to form a company and take over the management contract. It was an opportunity of a life-time and, of course, I agreed.

Sheraton was holding a world conference in New York and I along with all the general managers were invited to go down and participate. That week, John Hancock had decided that it was the appropriate time to cancel the contract.

Talk about timing! Right in the middle of the Sheraton world conference, a letter was sent to Sheraton terminating their management contract. All hell broke loose! Rather than be caught in the middle, I left New York to return to Boston. On the night of the main function for the Sheraton world conference, the president of Sheraton, Bud James, heard about the cancellation. His first words to his in-house attorney were, "Can we get the son-of-a-bitch deported?" Lawsuits started to fly and it became very unpleasant.

The John Hancock company in the meantime, was having more problems with its windows falling out, and I thought that they certainly didn't need any more bad publicity with the headlines that the canceling of Sheraton was creating.

However, much to my surprise I was called over to a board meeting at the John Hancock Tower and told that they would not back away from the situation, that I should stay put, and that they would work the problems out with Sheraton. Sure enough one month later l assumed the management, under the banner of my own company named Hotels of Distinction. Interestingly, when the attorney researched the name he found out that there had been a company of that name and would you believe, ran the Plaza in New York the Copley Plaza and a couple of other hotels including one in Cuba. What a good omen.

It is important to put a hotel on the map and make people think that it is the place to stay and be seen, I decided that was my top priority, we now had a first class property, beautifully decorated rooms, very fashionable and popular restaurants, which incidentally were setting a new trend. In the past guests had always dropped their suitcases and gone to local restaurants, now they were staying in the hotel because our restaurants were where the action was.

I decided to approach the theaters and artists agents and offer them very low rates to have the stars stay with us. They loved the idea and soon anyone who was playing in Boston stayed at our hotel.

Two of the first famous visitors were Elizabeth Taylor and Richard Burton. In fact they stayed with us on two occasions but they were a handful and taxed the employees to the limit.

We called the last of the three small rooms of Copley's, the Wine Room. At the end of that room was a sort of optical illusion, it was our wine storage for Copley's and with the aid of mirrors we had made it look as if there were rows and rows of bottles, instead of just a few rows, and it gave the room wonderful atmosphere. It became a favorite for private groups.

One night after a show Richard Burton wanted to have a cast party in the Wine Room. After a few drinks and half way through dinner Burton declared they were going to empty the wine cellar, and indeed they made a valiant effort. Unfortunately, Burton and Taylor got very drunk and very obnoxious. They got into an argument and created so much noise we had to threaten him with calling the police. They finally left and went off to bed at three a.m.

After they were divorced Elizabeth Taylor stayed with us on several occasions with her new husband, Senator John Warner. But at one point she and Burton were to appear in Noel Coward's play, "Private Lives." If I remember correctly it was her production, in any case her manager booked her in and we gave her the best suite in the Hotel.

However Burton's manager had also booked him into the hotel unbeknown to Liz Taylor, at least for a while. I had become quite friendly with her, and she always called me when she arrived in the hotel to thank me for the flowers or whatever we put in her room, so I was not surprised to receive a call from her. She asked me to come to the suite and when I arrived I think she had had a couple of drinks and was not in a pleasant frame of mind. I was greeted with "What the fuck do you mean by booking that SOB into this hotel? Either get him out or I leave with my entire group." I replied that I did not realize it would cause a problem. She replied, "Get him the fuck out of this Hotel."

An interesting problem.

At the time it was rumored that Burton was having an affair with the wife of a famous racing driver, so I went to see him. When he opened the door, I explained we may have a small problem, to which he roared with laughter and said, "What, the bitch doesn't want me in the same hotel, well you can tell her to go fuck herself. I could see why they had not been married for long. I looked at him innocently and said, "I am not sure what you are referring to, I just wanted to tell you Mr. and Mrs. racing car driver are checking in to the hotel tonight. As a precaution and I do not wish to be presumptuous, I booked you a suite at the Ritz, but you are of course welcome to stay here." He looked dumbfounded, said "Shit, I don't know what you have on your mind, but I don't want to stay in the same hotel as that bitch upstairs so I am off to the Ritz." One of the important traits a good hotelier must have is anticipation.

The crazy thing is I saw them a couple of nights later in Private Lives and they were so romantic the audience was crying.

Afterward Elizabeth Taylor dropped me a note saying, "Alan, it's good to be back in your wonderful hotel and I'm having much more fun this time."

Yul Brynner was another interesting character. He was appearing in the "King and I" at the Wilber Theater and stayed with us for two months. Before he arrived he sent us, through his manager, a list of 27 idiosyncrasies. For instance, he insisted eating only brown eggs. He had to have a special soap, only goose down pillows, etc.

When he arrived he asked to see me in his suite. First he asked if we had a freight elevator because he didn't want to be seen. I explained that we had a freight elevator but guests could not use it for insurance reasons. He then asked if I could get a case of 1966 Gauraud la Rose, a red Bordeaux wine. I explained we had a wonderful wine cellar which carried that wine, along with Chateau Gloria another Cordier wine that was a favorite of mine. Even though it was three o'clock in the afternoon he said lets share a bottle right now. I promptly ordered room service to bring a bottle and glasses up to his suite. He did this at his expense and we sat and enjoyed an hour of wine and interesting conversation.

The next morning I saw him exit the elevator all dressed in black, his shirt open to the waist and wearing a Stetson cowboy hat. So much for not being noticed. Anita and I became very friendly with him and his French wife. In fact we were having dinner with them both in our suite when he received news that he had adopted an Oriental baby.

He called me at 3 a.m. one morning with a problem. In that unmistakable voice he explained his wife was asleep in his suite but Kathy, his girlfriend, who I knew was down the hall was sick and needed a doctor. He asked if I would take care of the problem. Saul Cohen was the hotel doctor as well as my own personal physician. I called him and he came down and sorted things out. Brynner eventually divorced his wife and married Kathy, a dancer in the cast.

One late night security called me to say that Brad Davis, the actor, was screaming and sitting on the ledge outside his suite. When the security arrived the chain was on his door and I could not get him to answer. Again, I called Dr. Saul Cohen and had security cut the chain on the door and with the security guard went in and tried to talk him off the ledge and into the room,. He seemed to be out of his mind. Finally, ten minutes later Dr. Cohen arrived. In a joint effort we finally pulled him inside and got him onto the bed. Saul was examining him when I noticed at least ten bags from the Star Market scattered around the room, and they were full of whipped cream in aerosol cans. I pointed them out to Saul who questioned him about the cream. Davis said he was kinky and liked to take baths in whipped cream. However, Saul summarized that the actor was sniffing the gas from the cans and that's what caused his problem.

Not all our unusual clients were film stars. For instance Mary of Peter, Paul and Mary was a frequent visitor. Also a character who hung around the hotel every afternoon and evening. His name was John Dominic and fancied himself as a musician or, actually, a composer of music and would hang around with whoever was playing in the Hotel. But he was a bit of a mystery. He hung around the bar at Copley's, often with another character named Marty who claimed to be a film distributor but, for some reason or other, ended up going to jail for a few years. Dominic bought drinks for people but didn't drink himself. He always paid his bills in very old cash notes, and one day close to Christmas I saw him give something to my son and daughter. I asked them what it was and reluctantly they showed me he had given them each $500, all old one hundred dollar bills as a Christmas gift. I was concerned first because they were very old notes and I did not know if someone would ask question. So I took them over to the bank and said that my children had been given some money by an old uncle. The lady in the bank said they were from the 30's but were still good and gave me new notes.

Over the years I got to know John as well as I think anyone did. One day at least 10 years after I met him he asked me if I knew anyone who was a coin collector and through the Chamber of Congress I had met a dealer in coins etc., so I said yes. He said he had some $1000, and $500 bills and they were probably worth more than face value. He asked me if I would call this dealer and ask him if he would be interested. I did and the chap was so excited he said he would buy all the notes my friend had. I asked John how many did he want to trade. He shrugged and said, taking a roll from his pocket, how about 200 of each? As I repeated that into the phone I realized that that was $300,000. The coin dealer dropped the phone, and then said, "Forget it, this doesn't sound healthy." I agreed. Later John told me he sold those notes and a lot more to a Russian. Apart from this strange behavior he would also just disappear from the hotel for a few weeks and then turn up as if nothing happened. So who was he?

Another interesting story, my friend and attorney Ed had bought a property and built a small office building on Lewis Wharf which was considered to be in the north end. The building experienced a number of break-ins and then a visit from a gentleman who said he ran a security company and would take care of their security for a rather high fee. Ed talked to the Chief of police, who we both were friendly with, and they agreed to wire Ed's partner, and let him have another meeting with the security company. They also put a 2-hour watch on the offices.

At the second meeting the Italian gentleman repeated what he had said before, adding that they did not have to accept a high price and nor is there anything illegal in quoting high prices. Even with the police watch the building still got broken into and a whole bunch of computes were stolen.

Ed said to me maybe you could mention my problem to John Dominic, which I did over afternoon tea, John in his usual evasive way said he knew nothing about the north end or that sort of problem and then, after a sip of tea he asked if this was a good friend of mine who was having the problem. I replied yes and he immediately changed the subject and we talked about some jazz group that was to appear in the Merry Go Round bar. But, most mysteriously, from that day on nothing ever happened of a criminal nature in Ed's building. Who was John? I never really new. Many years after I left Boston, in my office in Palm Beach, I got a call from a person with a very raspy voice. He said that I may like to know that John Dominic had died. He added that there were no suspicious circumstances.

King Saudi of Saudi Arabia arrived one day at the Copley Plaza with two wives and a harem and took over a complete floor. They had asked that a partition be built blocking off the floor so no-one could enter their space and his security team posted guards at both ends.

The first problem we encountered was when the guards threw several mattresses out of the windows. They had evidently called house keeping to remove them and when they did not respond within half an hour, they removed them themselves.

Next day a maid reported that someone was cooking in the corridor. I was called and went up to see for myself. First of all the guards were not going to allow me to enter, after a little threatening conversation I was allowed to enter. I could not believe it, sure enough they were cooking over portable stoves and the corridor looked like a market place. I told them they couldn't do that and was told since they rented the whole floor they would do whatever they wanted. I simply called the fire department and they were closed down. One evening the king took over the Oval Room, and had a dinner where only 55 men were in attendance. He had a solid gold service flown in for the occasion.

On another occasion a party was given for Arthur Fiedler, the famous conductor of the Boston Pops Orchestra. The setting for the evening was in Venice and the ballroom was completely decorated in a Venetian theme complete with a canal filled with water on which a gondola floated across the ballroom. Later I had a fun lunch with Arthur Fiedler and Zsa Zsa Gabor and a local character by the name of Sonya Lowe, the wife of E.M. Lowe the movie theater owner. Mrs. Fiedler and Anita were also in attendance. Maestro Fiedler confessed he had snuck into see the movie "Deep Throat" in New York. Mrs. Fiedler did not understand the surprise on everyone's face. He explained to her that it was a story of a giraffe and laughed it off.

Zsa Zsa Gabor was playing at the Chateau De Ville and invited Anita and I to the first night. Honestly, I can't say that she was very good and a funny thing happened that first night. Evidently, when she was entering the stage during rehearsal she had tripped and fell and instead of pacifying her by sending her flowers, the owner of the Chateau De Ville insulted her to which she responded by calling him a Mafiosi. At the end of the performance of the first night an argument ensued and she stormed out of the theatre. Unfortunately my Bentley was parked outside and she threw herself onto the back seat. Anita and I drove her home and she bitched all the way. I told Zsa Zsa that it should not be an unpleasant evening since it was Anita's birthday. She immediately changed her mood and we all went back to the Merry Go Round and Zsa Zsa bought a bottle of Don Perignon champagne to celebrate Anita's birthday.

An interesting point is that most people think that film stars and personalities are unreachable when in actual fact they really can't go out in public to normal restaurants without being mobbed or at least inconvenienced. I found that they really enjoyed being invited up to our suite and entertained on a personal basis at a small dinner.

Some of the fun people I met were Thornton Wilder, a famous author, Joan Fontaine, Gene Shallit, Jean Dixon, Henny Youngman, a real fun character who often wrote me letters with his notorious one word per line. Anita and I also had dinner with Frank Sinatra whose son, when his father appeared at the Club, spent hours fixing our sound system and never charged me a dime.

Since we had so many stars and musicians coming through the hotel, Channel 5 suggested that I do a TV show from the hotel. It was called *Words and Music*. It, of course, did wonders for identifying the hotel in the local market. Joan Fontaine was one of the most interesting women I had on the program. It turned out she was not only married four times, which suggested that she was a good sport, but she was also a licensed interior designer, a fully licensed pilot, a Cordon Bleu chef and an experienced balloonist!

Yip Harburg was also an interesting interview. He was on the show with Mabel Mercer. Yip Harburg wrote, of course, *April In Paris, How Are Things In Glocca Mora, Over The Rainbow* and many other notable songs. Mabel Mercer was one of the greatest singers of all times in the night club circuit and taught Frank Sinatra how to enunciate.

An interesting but difficult man to interview was Joseph Levin, who produced *The Graduate* and *The Carpetbaggers.* Marty Brill was the most controversial. I interviewed him during the busing in Boston and asked him, "Since you have been charged with obscenity, what is the difference between obscenity and pornography?" To which he replied, "Obscenity is the word Nigger!" It was a live show and there was nothing much I could do. The producer signaled that I continue. They liked the fact that this was very controversial during this period. I am not sure that it was going to do much good for the hotel but I continued, and in fact nothing came of it.

Betty Condor and Alfred Adolph Green, who wrote the film scripts for *Singing In The Rain* and *Band Wagon,* were really a couple of characters. Theirs was a very lively show. Other musicians who came through were Stan Getz, Joanna Jones, Dizzy Gillespie, Sara Vaughn, Peter Nero, Dave Brubeck, Tony Bennett, Teddy Wilson and George Shearing who called me up one Sunday morning in the suite and asked me the best route that he could take down to the Cape where he would see the most scenery. Given the fact that he was blind, I asked him if he was pulling my leg. He said no. His wife drove and she explained to him everything on the way. Teddy Wilson played for quite some time in the bar. One day the housekeeper walked into my office and threw down a bunch of pornographic photos that had been found in Teddy Wilson's suite. Evidently he had made some remark to the maid and suggested she look at the photos. She ran out of the room crying and that had upset the housekeeper. I didn't really know what to do and I really thought that I should throw the photos away. Before I could do anything, Teddy Wilson appeared in my outer office asking my secretary if he could speak to me. I really did not want to embarrass him so I invited him into my office. When he told me that he was looking for some photos that had been taken from his suite I said I knew nothing about it but that I would look into it. We surreptitiously slipped the photographs into an envelope and pushed them under his door. Nothing further was said.

Ben Johnson was a character and always called down to Anita in the lobby, calling her Shirley Temple with her Louis Vuitton. He stayed at the hotel several times and one time he asked to see the newspapers the next morning so that he may see his reviews. David the head concierge went up to his suite the next morning and knocked on the door and there was no answer. He knocked two or three times and the maid came around the corner and as it happens so did the housekeeper. Just at that time, Ben Johnson opened the door. To everyone's surprise he was naked. Everyone was a little shocked, He said, "OK, so now you know I am a natural redhead."

My TV show ran for 12 weeks and ended with the most fantastic program that brought together Tony Bennett and Dave McKenna who was our resident pianist in the Plaza Bar. For a special fundraiser we had Count Basie and his band in the ballroom. It was a nationally syndicated program that gained a great deal of good publicity for the hotel.

Governor King was a frequent diner in our Cafe Plaza and I talked to him a couple of times about trying to attract movies into Boston since they were a good source of income for the hotel and indeed for the city and the state. He agreed and said that he would try to put together a film commission which he did and I was duly appointed chairman of the advisory committee. A young lady, the daughter of the state treasurer, Mary Lou Crane, was made the director of the Massachusetts Film Bureau and under her direction it became a great success.

For me, it was quite self-serving and I managed to bring into the hotel a number of films including The Brinks Robbery and A Small Circle of Friends. This activity developed some new friendships such as Peter Falk, Dino Di Laurentis as well as Burt Reynolds and Jill Clayberg. One night I had several drinks with Jill Clayberg in Copley's. I was surprised that she ended up drinking about 10 beers and asked me if I was impressed. I said I was very impressed that she drunk the 10 beers and not gone to the washroom.

Other interesting film personalities that I got to know very well were Peter Boyle, Paul Newman, Douglas Fairbanks, Jr., who used to call me all the time to book a special suite and even his dog Benji who came up and visited us and chased the cat around the apartment.

The Beatles stayed at one time in the hotel and, after separating as a group, John Lennon and Yoko Ono gave one of their famous interviews from the bed in their suite. It seemed a little ludicrous at the time because, after the press left, they insisted I sat there and talk to them while they remained in the bed. It was like visiting someone in the hospital.

Another interesting incident happened when there was a total blackout in the city of Boston and everybody was asked to remain in their rooms because it was dangerous to walk down the unlighted stairways. I got a terrified call from two ladies who said that there was a man in the suite next door threatening to kill everybody. I called security and we rushed up to the fifth floor to find out that an actor by the name of Roy Doutres was practicing his lines for "Death Trap" a play he was about to appear in, while walking up and down the corridor and of course terrifying all the local residents.

Another frequent visitor to the hotel was Myra Lansky, the famous Mafioso. At one point I was subpoenaed to go down to Miami with all his files, telephone bills, and folios. I didn't really want to go down to Miami. I went over to our Comptroller whose name was Jim D'Angelo and asked him if he would like a free trip to Miami and spend a couple of nights in a posh hotel. He thought that was a wonderful idea and asked what he had to do. I said simply go down with Myra Lansky's records and testify in court. And he said are you kidding? With a name like mine I'll never return. But he did.

For the movie industry Mary Lou Crane, Governor King, myself and an entourage went out to Hollywood to meet with producers who selected the sites for future movies. We traveled around promoting Massachusetts as a destination for film making. It was a great success and we brought more business to Massachusetts.

One of the films that we lured to Boston was "Yes, Giorgio", starring Luciano Pavarotti.

I had a guest appearance in the movie playing myself and had a lot of fun with the great singer. One afternoon after shooting he asked me where he could find the best lobster in Boston and I told him my apartment since I was having a birthday party for my wife Anita and he said, "Let's go." On arriving in the apartment, he sang happy birthday to Anita much to everyone's surprise and delight.

One day during the shooting of The Brinks Robbery, actor Peter Falk dressed up in one of the doorman's uniforms. He looked quite handsome and stood at the door for quite some time opening taxi cabs and car doors for people. Arriving guests said wow you look like the actor Peter Falk to which he replied, I am so sick of people saying that. I don't know who was more amused, them or him.

Some events were not quite as happy. More like nightmarish. Our attorneys were a Boston company called Masterman, Culbert and Tully. Ed Masterman is a personal friend and has been for some thirty years. Sometimes legal fees becomes a little difficult simply because my executive staff took the company and the lawyers for granted. The personnel director was calling out for advice and the members of the committee had other problems and the calls were becoming more numerous. So on March 26th, Ed Masterman called me and suggested that we have a drink and discuss our legal fees and other arrangements. We met in the Library Bar at 5:00 and over a couple of cocktails we discussed the problem. Ed Masterman suggested that although their company did not have any clients on retainer that maybe we should in fact pay them a retainer and that would give my executive staff and whoever else needed their services free access for at least a year and then we would see just how much time and hours were involved.

It seemed like an equitable solution and we came to a fee of $24,000 a year or $2000 a month. Confirming the agreement, I reiterated that this would give us full intents and purposes and restricted advice from their company within reason and he said that was correct so we shook hands on the deal – and had another drink. That night some nut lit eleven fires in various parts of the hotel. Two lives were lost and the damage ran into millions of dollars.

Ed Masterman was there at six o'clock the next morning since he heard it on the news. Half jokingly he said, "Were you aware of this before we made our arrangement last night?" That was the only humorous moment in the whole episode.

The phone rang at around 1:00 a.m. in my apartment and the operator said that there was a fire in the kitchen and that the alarms were going off. My wife awoke with the telephone and I suggested that she get Nathalie her daughter up who was living with us at the time. On crossing from one side of our apartment to the other she hurriedly came back and said that if the fire was in the kitchen we had a serious problem since there were flames outside our window.

I was dressed within a matter of seconds and covered everybody's faces with wet towels and got my wife and daughter down to the lobby as quickly as possible. Out staff had gone through a variety of fire drills and all those that were on duty were in the lobby awaiting instructions. Along with the security and everyone else we decided to evacuate the hotel, there was so much smoke and not knowing what damage was being done on the fifth floor. We instructed the telephone operators and the front desk personnel to call every room to ensure that everybody was in fact evacuating their rooms.

The fire department arrived in force and of course with flames coming out of the fifth floor windows it was indeed a full scale inferno. Guests were terrified. There is nothing worse than a fire. However, my staff acted sensationally and got everyone down off most of the floors into the lobby.

There were some amazing stories. Mrs. Edna Dryfus who lived on the fifth floor very close to our suite, she was around seventy-five years old and she had lived in the hotel for as long as I had. Evidently, on hearing the alarms she got dressed in her best night wear and found a bunch of guests wandering around not knowing which direction to go in the smoke. And the smoke in fact was now coming up through the stairwells. She made her way to the center of the building which was an E and she went down the center of the E and found the fire escape, led about 10 people down four floors onto a flat roof that abutted an office building next door. She evidently took off her high heeled shoe broke the window startling a security guard inside who then opened the window and led Mrs. Dryfus and her entourage through to safety.

In the center court of the hotel, people were trying to jump from the third of fourth floor onto the flat roof and, with a bull-horn I and some other staff told them to stay where they were because now the fire was confined to a specific area, however, several people did jump breaking their ankles and causing themselves quite a bit of harm.

I had been up talking to the fire department and found out that the fire was contained in fact to the area underneath where I lived. It was a suite occupied by Sumner Redstone, the theater mogul, and a young woman. Next door was an associate of his and another young woman. Both unfortunately perished in the fire. Sumner Redstone survived with serious bums. His young lady friend escaped from the ledge down the fire ladder.

The fire was actually contained on the fifth floor in one section. The hotel was built like a castle with thick walls, terra cotta floors and ceilings, smoke doors, and in fact was a very safe property even though at the time it did not have sprinklers.

Discussing later the incident with the fire department it was thought the fire was lit outside the suite 541, Sumner Redstone's suite and a sofa had been put in front of the door or close to the door. It was a total mystery because no furniture was left in the corridor and must have been taken from another suite. One thing is for sure though if they had not opened the door, no one would have been badly harmed and one should always remember whether you are in a hotel or your own home if there is a fire outside to feel the door and not open the door if it is hot.

Another amusing incident, if one can call anything amusing during a fire, a friend of mine was having a convention in the city at the Sheraton Boston, a 1500 room hotel across the city. He preferred to stay with me in a more elegant hotel and in one of my suites. Unfortunately he had to evacuate the hotel being taken off the ledge of the hotel by a fire truck. His senior vice presidents were watching the fire on television and realized that Joe Venucci was in my hotel so they rushed across and met him in the lobby and immediately took him back to the presidential suite at the Sheraton Boston. While everyone was sitting around in the Sheraton Boston having a drink to calm Joe's nerves, someone said that Joe really smelled of smoke and he should probably go and take a shower. Then, all of a sudden, the fire alarm went off and the lights went out. and the same maniac that had lit the fires in the Copley Plaza had lit several fires in the Sheraton Boston. Joe Venucci along with all his friends had to walk down 28 floors and sit in the lobby. Believe it or not, Joe Venucci returned to the Copley Plaza later that evening and went back to his suite in the hotel.

My old friend and contractor Paul Perela turned up at five o'clock in the morning with his crew along with other crews that were experienced in getting rid of the smell of smoke and cleaning up. We had locked off the fifth floor and by 10 o'clock cleaned up the hotel.

You never would have believed that a fire had happened in the hotel the previous evening.

Everyone who checked into the hotel was told that there was a fire the night before, but there were no concerns and the hotel was perfectly safe. After that the city of course tightened up on the fire life safety requirements and a much more sensitive fire alarm system was put into the hotel. Unfortunately very sensitive and it seemed to go off every second or third night at the most unfortunate times waking everyone up in the hotel and I was now out of bed within seconds and in the lobby. It was my resident manager, Bill Heck, telling everyone it was a false alarm.

One night we had a group in the hotel that sold lingerie nationwide. It was one of these groups that trained local young housewives who then went out and had demonstrations in their homes. However, on this particular evening, there were sixty young ladies staying in the hotel and the fire alarm went off about one o'clock in the morning. Fifty young ladies in the most exotic underwear and nightwear that you had ever seen ended up in the lobby much to the amusement and delight of the firemen.

The hotel was the scene of some of the most spectacular parties. Some put on by the hotel as promotion, others put on by companies, clients and eccentrics. One such eccentric party was almost a fiasco. Someone had been to the Arthur Fiedler party and seen how we had created a Venetian Canal the length of the ballroom. It was their mother's 80th birthday and they wanted the same scene created with a table on one end of the ballroom which was the reception area and a sort of throne seat at the other end of the ballroom on the stage. Someone would then punt a gondola down the full length of the ballroom with her in the seat of honor, whilst forty violinists stood in the eight balconies around the mezzanine floor playing the sound of music. She would then be carried to a chair on the stage whilst everyone sang happy birthday. And indeed the ballroom was set up magnificently. The question was who could we find that looked magnificent to punt the gondola and carry the old lady to her seat?

While touring the hotel with a client, we had gone through the kitchen to visit with the chef and discuss a special menu and in doing so we had passed the silver room where the silver was cleaned and there in magnificent splendor was a black gentleman stripped to the waist in a pair of red parachute pants covered in silver powder. He looked so magnificent with all the silver powder over him and he was such a big man that the client said why can't we use him and dress him up like Othello and to be quite honest, I didn't know why we couldn't if he was willing. I didn't know the employee, but saw no reason why we couldn't employ him for the evening to do this particular event.

I talked to the personnel director the next morning and we visited the gentleman concerned. He was not very bright. He was extremely big. He didn't quite understand what we wanted, but agreed to do it when a handsome fee was offered. We rented a costume for him that looked very much like Othello. We also showed him how to punt the Gondola, and carefully lift the Lady on to the chair. Simple? Right!

On the night of the evening, the gentleman concerned was very nervous about what he was doing and unbeknownst to all of us, was having a few drinks to fortify his nerves. At the prescribed time we got him and the lady into the gondola. As the violinists began to play, he started to punt her up the ballroom. As he neared the stage, as he had been told, he put down his punt, walked along the gondola and picked up the old lady. Carefully, I might add. As he was about to step out of the gondola onto the stage someone got their cues mixed and Othello stood there on the bow of the punt, holding the old lady and refusing to step out of the punt. He froze, thinking he was going to fall into the water. The violinists played on. We beckoned him from the sides of the stages indicating that he should step out of the gondola. He stood there with his eyes as wide and as white as plates. The old lady was terrified, not knowing what to do, and he was starting to hurt her by holding her too tight. This was when John Cronis, our banquet manager, stepped forward to grab him and pull him and the old lady onto the stage thus averting a disaster. The old lady was a little shaken but other than that the event went off smoothly.

We decided to put on a party for the 50th anniversary of prohibition. I thought it would be a fun, unique party and we decided to turn the ballroom into a speakeasy. We hung factory lights from the ceiling, fixtures with green shades and big bulbs. We built a bar a hundred feet long and filled a bathtub full of gin. Comedian Henny Youngman was hired to entertain and we found a stripper who would lie in a coffin and be carried in by six pallbearers down a runway in the middle of the ballroom The coffin was meant to represent the end of prohibition. We invited only males to the party which annoyed a lot of local people but that was the idea. We even told the television crews that were going to cover the function that they could not send any women. This really got the feminists uptight. Unbeknown to many of the businessmen who were attending the function that night, we had asked their wives to come dressed as "ladies of the night", in other words as hookers. Believe me they really went all out and did an incredible job. There was a wonderful local comedian by the name of Lannie and she organized the group of wives and other female clients. She gave them placards and at a pre-determined time crashed the event in the ballroom and they acted as a group of very annoyed feminists. Of course all this happened just as the television crews arrived. Once again, we hit national television.

Another marvelous event was the hotel's 75th anniversary. I decided that it was time for the hotel to be recognized as the grand old dame that she was and we dressed all the staff and employees in costumes of the 1912 era, when the hotel was opened. With the addition of a lot more palms and flowers and a friend of mine lent me two 1912 Rolls Royce Silver Ghosts which were parked in the lobby. Everything looked sensational. Menus were faithfully reproduced even down to the 1912 prices and the public was invited to participate. We rented out rooms at $3.50 a night and suites for $5, mainly to our corporate clients and friends.

Again, the event captured national television and in fact it was not that expensive to do. After all, the restaurants could only seat 250 and even if you turn them over for two sittings for both lunch and dinner, it was not that much we were giving away. The bars were packed because we were selling drinks for 35 cents which was in fact probably our cost and the media coverage could not have been bought.

Another source of income were weddings held or performed in the Oval Room and at the famous local Trinity church next door. But everyone wanted something different. For instance, the Young President's Organization came to see me to find out what we could do that was different. Basically, they wanted a wonderful dinner and dancing for about 150 couples but they did not want to hire the typical band, even if it was Lester Lanin or Peter Duchin. I suggested almost jokingly what about the Boston Pops? And they thought that was a marvelous idea. It cost $30,000 to hire the Pops for one evening and it took us two days to construct a special stage with lighting and sound but according to the organizers, it was the finest party they had ever had.

Another guest who I knew very well and who was getting married wanted something extremely exotic and very different. I suggested that we could dress the ballroom up with a huge tent and reproduce A-thousand-and-one-nights theme. He thought that was a great idea. We totally tented the ballroom which was 6,000 square feet. It was 30 feet high and all in silk. The ceiling had eight magnificent 8-foot crystal chandeliers which we hung through the silk canopy.

The walls were simply like a tent and the tables were in rows on the floor, two feet of the floor were covered with cushions as seats to lounge on. The tables were filled with food and we hired twenty belly dancers to dance up and down the tables during the meal. It cost the host a fortune, but he went away more than happy.

Another of the great parties that I organized was for Prince Charles when he was visiting Boston. The local British consulate, David Bums, wanted to have a party for Prince Charles but didn't know how it could be carried off with so many different factions in Boston having to be invited, including the politicians, the socialites, etc. I suggested that we could set up the ballroom as a Buckingham Palace type lawn party and that we would divide the ballroom into various sections with loads and loads of flowers and we would station all these various interest groups in their different areas and then bring Prince Charles around to visit with each of the groups. Everyone thought that was a great idea. Prince Charles' personal secretary, however, said that that was impossible because Prince Charles would stand at the door of the ballroom and shake hands with everybody as they came in. This was the normal procedure and one that was accepted by security of the palace. After many what seemed hours of discussion I finally convinced them that what we suggested was really the most elegant way of doing it and I ensured him we would carry it off well. And finally he agreed. The invitation list was almost 1000 people. Anyone who was anyone in the city of Boston and the details got more complicated as we went along. Scotland Yard was involved as well as the FBI. The FBI told me that only half an hour before the function was going to begin that they would sweep the ballroom for bombs and such. They would have their dogs sniff and then no one would be allowed into the ballroom until the Prince arrived. I explained to them that that was not possible. The ballroom was going to be filled with a thousand people and then the Prince was going to come in. Another argument ensued and finally they agreed to do it my way.

The representative of the Scotland Yard team was a gentleman by the name of Carruthers who spoke with a wonderful British accent. Unbeknown to me, a local radio personality by the name of Jess Kane, a very good friend of mine, was listening to me while I was talking to the gentleman from Scotland Yard and decided to play a little joke on me. I was in a staff meeting going over all the final details when the phone rang and Sergeant Carruthers came on the phone. He explained to me that he was standing in the ballroom and that there were all these green plants and flowers around. I said I knew that, it had taken us two days to set it up. And he said, but that's impossible, Prince Charles was allergic to green plants and flowers and they would have to be removed. Of course, this was only an hour before Prince Charles was due to arrive. I almost went crazy and told him that was an absolute impossibility and that Prince Charles would just have to have a stiff upper lip and go through with the program, at which point Jess Kane, who had been taking off the accent of Carruthers, exploded in laughter. I could have killed him.

The event was an enormous success. I met Prince Charles with the British consul at the front door and he was led down Peacock Alley which was the entrance to the hotel escorted by the tenth regiment as an honor guard and in the lobby the ancient and honorable artillery military group was also stationed and he was led into the ballroom. He loved the idea of people in different groups and spending time with them and in fact called me the next morning and asked me to go up to his suite where he told me that if he had anything to do with it this is how it was going to be done in the future, not be standing in line for ages and ages shaking everybody's hand and not having any time to socialize.

They say it is the oldest profession in the world, but I think the hotel is since she obviously needed somewhere to take her clients. Believe me it's still going on today.

Evidently, Mr. Jones in 411 picked himself up a rather attractive lady in a local bar downtown, got very drunk and brought her back to the hotel. She agreed to stay the night and both being quite drunk, fell soundly asleep. In the morning, he awoke to find her beside him covered in blood, apparently with her throat cut. He went into an absolute panic, checked out of the hotel and left the poor woman in bed. A rather traumatic experience for the maid who found her and called security who then called me and the police. It was, to say the least, a gruesome sight.

When the police doctor examined the woman, he found that she had had some sort of throat operation and a plug inserted in her throat. Probably because she was drunk, she had somehow choked during the night, dislodged the plug and drowned in her own blood. I had no idea what happened to her roommate whose name was clearly identified on his check-in slip. He obviously wasn't going to be difficult to track down. It's unfortunate that he panicked and left her in the state she was in. I'm sure that he had a lot of explaining to do when he got home. It's hard to believe what people will complain about, but a gentleman turned up in my office saying that he had been robbed the night before in the hotel, not only of his money and credit cards but of some of his clothes. I asked him to explain a little further. He was outraged that we would allow *those* types of people into the hotel. I, on the other hand, had a terrible problem keeping a straight face. "What sort of hotel are you running?" he asked.

Evidently, he had been in the bar and solicited by a young attractive woman who he agreed to take to his room. Just as they were getting undressed, there was a knock at the door and another rather attractive, but much younger woman by the name of Jenny was waiting outside. The older one of the two explained that she was in some sort of training and if he didn't object the other young girl would watch and maybe join in at no cost, just to get some experience. Evidently, he could resist anything but temptation and he let the young lady in. Unfortunately, after he got undressed and into bed with the older women, the younger one took off with not only his pants, but his wallet as well. The older woman, not quite dressed, said she was appalled and chased after the younger woman. Of course, it was a perfect scam and he was left in a rather embarrassing situation. Not only was he out of money and credit cards, but he had to charge a new pair of pants to his hotel bill. He was insisting that I do something about it. I suggested that perhaps I would look into it. I told him that I was sure I had his home address on his registration card and that I would be more than happy to write to him to try to compensate him in some way. At this time he again panicked and said, "No, don't write to anybody just let me get out of here." Of course, he would never return.

Problems were caused by young women who were either picked up in the bar or picked up clients at the bar and came back to the hotel. A much more serious problem, and one that was almost unsolvable, was the call girls (the more expensive ones) who got into the hotel. The truth of the matter was that the profile of the call girl had changed dramatically and, for the most part, created no problems. Furthermore, they couldn't be easily caught. They were run by a sophisticated young lawyer around 35 years old who was quite well known in the city of Boston. He could always be seen walking around my hotel or that of the Ritz or the Four Seasons with his coat over his shoulders like a real dandy. With a little cooperation, we found out he was running a string of young women who would be in the lobby by the public telephones of which there were several locations at the time the guest checked in. Upon checking in, the guest was given a message to call this number which he did and the young lady appeared beside him at the desk or very shortly in his room after he checked in. We discovered that it was this lawyer simply because he solicited a very attractive wife of a friend of mine who was having afternoon tea by herself in the hotel. He joined her at the table and then proceeded to suggest that there were ways she could make money during the afternoon while her husband was at work. He even gave her a business card. We thought it would be a good idea if she called and we could somehow trap him into giving us the information that we needed. However, he apparently caught on because he never contacted her when she called his office. His secretary simply said that he was unavailable.

Two guests I knew very well were in the hotel at least twice a month and used these services. Of course it wasn't in my best interest to question them because I knew them well and they were very good clients of the hotel. One was an impeccably dressed gentleman in his 60's who, in his early days, was in the diamond business and in his later days became president of one of the local Boston banks. He would appear in the main dining room at least twice a week with a very gorgeous young woman in her mid-twenties. The other man was a movie distributor whose tastes were a little more bizarre. He would go for the Ethiopian or the East Indian. He once told me that he was trying to work his way through the United Nations.

The most bizarre story of all was with a friend of mine and another good client of the hotel. He was a character, not unlike Burl Ives, the burly actor and of course a New Yorker. He was married to a very intelligent woman who worked for the United Nations. We'll call him Bill. Bill was in his sixties and had had a series of heart attacks. He had left everything to his wife or had put everything in her name. Unfortunately, when he was in the hotel one day, he got a message that his wife had fallen off a horse and had gone into a coma. She later died and Bill was devastated. Every time you talked about his wife, he would cry and say that after all these heart attacks, he would be gone very soon. He, in fact, left me his Rolls Royce which I didn't need (I couldn't afford the one I was running) and made me the executor of his will.

About three months after his wife died, he was in the hotel having a drink in the small library bar with my wife Anita and her daughter Nathalie. We were going to discuss going to Machu Picchu in Peru. I had gone over to the men's room which was at the other end of the hotel and had run into a Rolls Royce dealer from New York. He was one of those that checked in and got a message. Shortly thereafter he was met by a young attractive woman. In this particular case I had seen the woman in the hotel on several occasions with various clients including the distinguished old gentleman who used to come in the main dining room once or twice a week. I knew who she was and I knew who the client was. I spoke to them and went back across the lobby to find my wife and daughter and Bill. Bill had decided also to go to the men's room. The young lady, we shall call Pamela, had decided to follow me to ask me something which she did just as we all came together in the middle of the lobby. I had no option but to introduce her to Bill. Bill asked her if she would like to join us for a drink in the Library Bar, something I was not too thrilled about because it wasn't exactly wise to have a call girl join my wife and daughter for a drink, but there was very little I could do. And she did in fact join us. Prior to her joining us, Bill had said that he would love to join us on our trip to Peru. I had explained to him that if he had had four or five heart attacks, going up to the heights that you had to reach Machu Picchu was not a very good idea. But he was very keen to do something with us and much to my surprise in explaining this to young Pamela, he asked her if she would like to join us on the trip. Wonderful! We were now going to go on vacation with a call girl!

To cut a long story short, we were all going to Peru, and something happened to the airplane as we were leaving Boston some weeks later. Our flight was delayed and we missed the connection to Peru. However, Bill and Pamela did go off to Machu Picchu. They had a wonderful trip and on their return got married and disappeared from our lives.

Some months later, in attending a fancy dress ball at The Breakers in Palm Beach, Anita said to me, "Do you know who that beautiful blonde is up on the stage?" I looked and said, "No, but I wouldn't mind knowing who it is." "That is Pamela Herman," she replied. I couldn't believe it. When she went back to the table, sure enough there was Bill, sitting amongst the Palm Beach socialites! I went over to talk to him, but he was very upset that I had recognized him and his wife. He presumably thought that I was going to tell everyone what his wife was. I had no such intentions, but he was very agitated. Later, he came over and apologized. He explained that they had moved to Palm Beach and they had become very social (he had given a Cadillac to this particular function). My reaction was, "congratulations!"

An interesting conclusion to the story is that if she married him for his money, she had to put up with him for a long time because he lived for another 25 years and she was 26 or so when she met him and recently acquired his 1972 Rolls Royce and I hope some money.

Before the advent of the plastic key, hotels were an open invitation to smalltime robbers. Guests at the Copley would unwittingly or carelessly drop their keys into ashtrays or wooden boxes at the door. The keys would then be retrieved, sat on for a few days and used to get back into the rooms. Inside jobs were prevalent with the maid tipping off her boyfriend as to what was in the room of any value. And believe me, guests would leave jewelry, cameras and cash sitting on top of the dressers, which was a great temptation for someone earning not much more than $4 an hour.

Robberies come in all shapes and sizes, including the two black girls who worked the check rooms around the city. One would check a mink or sable coat and receive a ticket. Later in the evening she would return to the check room saying that she had lost her ticket, but would say, "That's my coat over there. Here's my driver's license with my picture on it. My name is written or embroidered inside on the coat lining and there's a credit card in the pocket with my name on it." Sure enough, the poor unsuspecting check girl would check all this and find out that in fact it was true and give her the coat. Of course, when her accomplice, having been given the ticket, later turned up and there was no mink coat, a claim against the hotel would follow. Small time larceny but extremely aggravating.

During yet another incident, the security guard called me to

219

explain that an Arabian sheik had lost $50,000 worth of jewelry that he was carrying in his briefcase. I went up to the suite and met with the gentleman. He explained to me that he had left his briefcase in the suite. Someone had come into the suite, opened the briefcase and stolen the diamonds. I explained to him that our insurance company would no doubt take care of this, but that I needed a receipt showing that he had declared these diamonds coming into the country, which was the law. He looked at me and muttered for quite a few minutes in some foreign tongue. Then, he asked me to get out of his suite. Obviously, he had not declared the diamonds coming into the country, or perhaps they had never been stolen, but nothing further was heard. One day a jewelry show had been booked in the ballroom and my wife wanted to go around and see the displays. We spent a nice Sunday afternoon touring around the various booths. As we were passing by one booth, I saw a gentleman wearing the worst looking shirt that I had ever seen, a purple and green, sort of muddled design. As I was looking at his shirt in distaste, he pinched the bottom of the blonde assistant who was working in his booth. She sort of giggled and slapped his hand, with all this taking place in a matter of seconds. Other than that display, we enjoyed the show. Luckily, I didn't have to buy anything. The next morning, a gentleman appeared in my office in a suit saying that he had been robbed. It was very strange because, as soon as he walked into my office, I recognized him as the man in the hideous shirt. I listened to his complaint and asked him if anyone besides himself had been in his suite. He said, "No, absolutely not." I told him I would review the matter and get back to him within the hour. I decided to see if I could bluff him. I went up to his suite and told him that in reviewing the security cameras, we had noticed that a blonde woman had entered into his suite the evening before. He was absolutely furious and asked me if this was a general practice of the hotel to videotape everything that went on in the hotel. I explained to him it was only for security reasons and that only the elevators and corridors were monitored. In actual fact, they were not! He became very flustered. He said, "Well, maybe she did enter the room and I didn't see her. Maybe she did have a key. I'll have to check that." Henceforth, we never heard anything more.

Phillip's Auctioneering House was going to hold one of the largest auctions in the history of Boston with a lot of modern and contemporary art. We were asked to provide double the security that we normally did and the room and doors were covered with security cameras. The auction took place on a Friday and was a roaring success. The ballroom was cleared and Saturday night was the night of a rock concert. On Monday morning, I got a very embarrassed call from Phillip's who said that they had sold a Calder mobile valued at $80,000 but unfortunately couldn't find it. They were wondering if it may still be hanging on the stage in the ballroom and asked if I would please check. We checked the ballroom and the stage to no avail. Phillip's was highly embarrassed that they had lost a Calder mobile which the customer had already paid for.

A few days later a young engineer appeared in my office and asked if I was looking for something that had been hanging on the stage. I immediately replied that we were. He suggested that it may be something he found which he had in the boiler room. We proceeded to go down to the basement and to the boiler room. Sure enough, there it was hanging on one of the pipes - the missing Calder mobile. The crazy part was that it had survived through a prom night with a rock band on the stage. On Sunday there had been a Jewish wedding with the place of ceremony set on the stage. The engineer had taken it down and hung it in the boiler room, thinking that it would be a fun thing to take home to his kids. Luckily, he didn't. Phillip's was most relieved to get their mobile back with no damage done.

I think it was Barnum & Bailey who said, "It doesn't matter what the publicity is, so long as you get the name right," and that in fact is true. Sometimes when you get a large robbery, it really doesn't do the hotel any harm. In fact, it makes the hotel out to be a glamorous place because of the people who were staying there and the exciting event that had happened.

Actor, Peter Falk, while playing in the movie Brinks Robbery, which was partly shot at the Copley Plaza, had to dress as a hotel doorman. As a joke, between takes, he surprised hotel guests by opening their car doors and ushering them into the hotel. Many guests said, "You know, you look just like Peter Falk." "Yes," he answered, "I get that all the time."

Curt Gowdie, famed sports announcer, was a frequent guest and good friend of General Manager Tremain.

Actor Sebastian Cabot became friends with Tremain over their mutual love for cars.

Richard Burton and Elizabeth Taylor, when they were first married in Canada.

THE COPLEY PLAZA
COPLEY SQUARE, BOSTON, MASSACHUSETTS 02116

ALAN TREMAIN
MANAGING DIRECTOR

February 14, 1977

Mrs. John Warner
Copley Plaza Hotel
John Hancock Suite
Room 531/3

Dear Mrs. Warner:

With reference to our brief discussion on Friday, enclosed
are some press clippings from your last visit to the Copley
Plaza. I hope you will find them interesting.

Since they are an important part of our hotel's history, I
would appreciate you returning them to us. If you would
call extension 166, my secretary, Marilyn, would be more
than happy to pick them up.

Yours sincerely,

ALAN TREMAIN
Managing Director

AT/mrc

To Alan T.
Thanks you for your hospita-
— I'm having much
more fun this
time! Best alwa

TELEPHONE (617) 267-5300

OPERATED BY HOTELS OF DISTINCTION, INC.

Letter from Elizabeth after she married Senator John Warner.

225

Mr. And Mrs. Yul Brynner – famous guests at the Copley Plaza.

Tony Bennett, singer, and pianist and composer Dave McKenna,
worked together on Alan's TV show called "Words & Music."

THE COPLEY PLAZA
COPLEY SQUARE, BOSTON, MASSACHUSETTS 02116

Friday morning
March 14 1975

Dear Mr Tremain :
May thanks for your kind expression of welcome. I'm had — again — a delightful visit at the Copley-Plaza.
Please thank, too Mr Armen and Mr Todhunter also for making my visit pleasant

Sincerely yours

Thornton Wilder

#421

Letter of thanks from author Thornton Wilder.

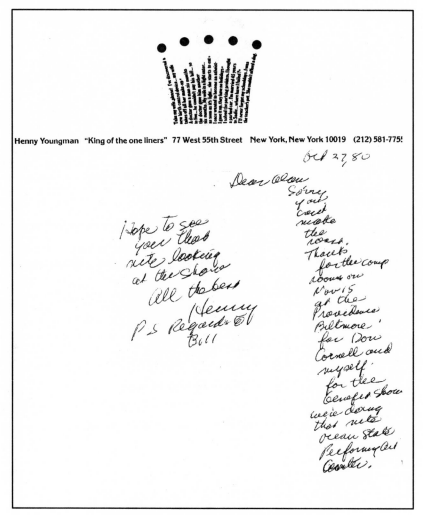

Henny Youngman "King of the one liners" 77 West 55th Street New York, New York 10019 (212) 581-775!

King of the one-liner, Henny Youngman,
writes a letter of thanks to Alan – in one-liners.

Zsa Zsa Gabor in all her beauty.

Alan Tremain appeared as himself with Luciano Pavarotti in the movie, "Yes, Giorgio."

*Here is the world's most famous tenor with Tremain
at the Copley Plaza.*

Tremain entertains Vanessa Redgrave and her daughter in the Café Plaza.

General Manager, Tremain, greets Prince Charles of England during his visit to America in 1986.

CHAPTER TWENTY FIVE

Recession: A Buyers Market

On January 18, 1984, the following article appeared in the Banker & Tradesman. Its headline said:

Copley Plaza's Tremain called in to revive ailing Back Bay Hilton Hotel

"It's not easy running a hotel in Boston these days, as the owners of the Back Bay Hilton can attest.

Their 372-room hotel, towering over the Back Bay from Dalton Street, opened in October 1982, about the same time several other new hotels – the Meridian, the Long Wharf Marriott and the Bostonian – came on the market.

It was a bumper crop, planted by a mayor who promised that the new hotel rooms would be harvested quickly by conventioneers coming to Boston's enlarged convention center.

Today, that mayor, Kevin White, is gone from office; the Hynes Auditorium has yet to be expanded; and one of the new hotels, the Back Bay Hilton, has just escaped what some said was near-disaster.

On January 5th, the John Hancock Mutual Life Insurance Co., until then majority owner in the hotel, announced that it had taken full control of the hotel and had installed new management. The announcement, while not surprising to those who were aware of the Hilton's vacancy rates, served as a chilling reminder that the promises of a hot hotel market in Boston have not been borne out.

But the man who took over the management of the Hilton doesn't appear to be worried, either about the future of that hotel or the market in general, as he moves to make changes on Dalton Street.

Alan Tremain, the debonair keeper of the Copley Plaza Hotel for the past 12 years and president of Hotels of Distinction, named by John Hancock to run the Hilton, believes the turmoil in the market now will be followed by halcyon days."

Within months of opening a very unique restaurant and bar called "Boodles" the hotel became the place to be seen. Rave reviews in the local press helped pack the restaurant and bar, and also overflowed the room occupancy.

Also, despite a recession the Copley Plaza was way ahead of its competition in both occupancy and rate. Every day or two the Hotel Association circulated the major hotels statistics, so we knew what and how everyone was doing. And, according to rumor, some were in financial trouble.

It was a tempting time to think some properties may be for sale at bargain prices. As it was constructed, my company earned its income from management fees which we lived off. I needed a fairy godmother – with deep pockets.

Just about every Monday I had lunch with Arthur Kinder one of the John Hancock Realty Division executives. He just liked to hear how the hotel was doing and enjoyed a good lunch in the Café Plaza, our gourmet restaurant. On one particular Monday in November of 1983 Bill Leary, the Chairman of the John Hancock Realty Division decided to join us. We were good friends and went to quite a few local social functions together with our wives. He explained that they had the mortgage on the fairly new 340-room Back Bay Hilton which was having serious financial problems. The owners were behind on their payments and Hancock had decided to take it back. Basically, it was a foreclosure.

What did I think about managing it for them? I knew the hotel well, the owner Bob Sage was a good friend. I declared that it was a good property but very bland. It had nice rooms but a mediocre restaurant and was no match for the competition which were also having problems, therefore lowering room rates and offering all sorts of deals.

I said that I would love to take it over. I had built a fabulous management team at the Copley and we had the resources. I added that I would need to devise a new concept for the restaurant, something that would attract the theater crowd since it was next to a popular movie theater.

He agreed and asked me to put together a budget. One month later my company took over the management with a five year contract. The timing was perfect. January was a quiet time in Boston. We closed the restaurant and decided something casual would be appropriate. I came up with the name, "Boodles" which had been a famous club in London a long time ago. The idea was to create an atmosphere that was clubby but also a little bit of a French Bistro. I went on a treasure hunt buying all sorts of old pictures and photos of old Boston. We plastered the walls with them and it was very eclectic. I also found a bunch of handsome wall sconces and chandeliers that were from an old Stouffers Restaurant. We added antique chairs and it looked like it had been there for years. Very comfortable looking.

On St. Patrick's Day I had an opening party to which we invited about a hundred and fifty local business and potential customers. I had a friend called Bill Burnham who booked musical acts into clubs in New York. He had helped me with the Plaza Bar at the Copley so I asked him to find someone special to be a sort of star attraction. He came up with Sebastian Cabot with whom we had worked before and he was a great success.

We found we had another success on our hands, despite the continuing recession. Occupancy in the hotel increased with corporate bookings and Boodles was packed almost every day. Within six months the hotel was turning a profit. In Hancock's view I could do nothing wrong.

CHAPTER TWENTY SIX

Deal Maker

With the recession deepening there were some great deals out there and I needed some more deep pockets.

I approached a well-known investment banker, James Caper and met in London with two gurus, Christopher Henderson and Ralph Di Fiori. Together we did a dog and pony show and convinced six American and one British pension fund to put up $56 million.

Here is an article in the local press entitled **Dealmaker**.

"It's been a stomach-wrenching ride to the bottom for the hotel industry.

Overbuilding, a slow economy and a travel slump caused by the Persian Gulf War combined to drive hotel occupancy nationwide to an all-time low in 1991. Room rates haven't kept up with inflation. Seven out of 10 hotels and motels nationally are running in the red, according to KMPG Peat Marwick.

Still, with the hospitality industry in its worst shape in decades, Tremain's Hotels of Distinction has been buying. It has a plan.

'What they're doing is capitalizing on the times,' says Sheldon Greene, of Miami-based hotel broker Sheldon Greene & Associates Inc, 'They're very able very sharp. I do believe it's the way to go. I think Tremain is in there at the right time.

A typical buy was the 275-room Sheraton Needham outside Boston, a 4-year-old hotel that cost $34 million to build. Tremain's company bought it in December from the Resolution Trust Corp. for $11 million."

I had developed quite a reputation and the name, Hotels of Distinction, was getting well known with numerous articles in local, national and trade press. I started to receive phone calls from brokers and owners that had troubled properties. Most wanted to sell and could not afford a management contract but I did not have the financial resources.

Through other business negotiations I had met a fellow Englishman named Chris Henderson who worked for an investment bank called James Capel, based in London. Because of the publicity I was receiving and my connection with China during my days at the Peninsular Hotel in Hong Kong, he asked me if I would be interested in becoming director of a newly listed fund called The China Fund that was going to invest in that country. I said I would love to and subsequently met in New York with other potential directors. They included a retired British Ambassador to China, Sir Alan Donald, an American attorney with Hughes, Hubbard and Reed who lived and practiced in France, Mike Holland, a well known investment banker in New York with connections with the State Street Bank, Joe Rogers, an investment banker and director of the Taiwan Fund, Nigel Tulloch and Australian director with the Hong Kong Shanghai Bank. An impressive group.

I could not believe that at our first meeting I was nominated the Chairman of the Board.

Partly through these new connections I met with Chris Henderson and two colleagues, James Capel and Ralph Di Fiori. We put together what is called a dog and pony show with the sole purpose of raising funds to buy hotels. To do so we visited several British and American pension funds. Our efforts resulted in raising $56 million.

For me it was a very different ball game, as they say. I was now in the acquisition business, not actually running the hotels but remaining very involved with day to day operations – which made for long days.

A typical purchase was the Sheraton in Needham just outside Boston. A four year old property that cost $34 million to build but had defaulted on its obligations and taken over by the Resolution Trust, a government agency. We bought it for $11 million.

I went on to purchase the Albuquerque Hilton in New Mexico, a thousand room hotel in Montreal and a small hotel in Palm Beach, Florida – something to play with in the winter. I loved Palm Beach and ended up buying a fabulous apartment in the Esperante Building and so began a new life. Over the years I had been married and divorced three times – but that's another story.

I decided to live full time in Palm Beach and leave the day to day chores to a very professional management team. I intended to enjoy life. Luckily, I met a gorgeous and wonderful woman called Ingrid who had the sweetest disposition. We married and, as they say, lived happily ever after.

Chapter Twenty Seven

The Finale
Command Performance

B ecause of my past experiences in China and my business acumen, the principles of James Caper asked me to be the Chairman of the newly formed "The China Fund." A position I held for 10 years.

As the press and Noel Coward observed in one of his songs an unconventional Englishman can apparently catch the attention of powerful people in high places. One day a letter arrived.

> *Sir,*
> *"I am commanded to inform you that an investiture will be held at Buckingham Palace at which your attendance is requested, etc"*

It was a great honor to receive from the Queen of England the title, "Officer of the most excellent order of the British Empire, a class of knighthood."

An article in a financial newspaper read:

KNIGHT OF HOSPITALITY

An officer of the Most Excellent Order of the British Empire, Tremain spent 17 years before 1989 running Boston's historic Copley Plaza Hotel. He used his international contacts and social and business acumen to turn the Copley from a faltering property into a lucrative draw for the prosperous and photogenic.

He entertained Prince Charles in his private quarters in the hotel. The wall of his Palm Beach office is cluttered with photographs of movie, opera, business and government notables from that heady time. Tremain became a celebrity. He had a television talk show, he represented the Boston hotel industry in negotiating with labor for nearly 10 years and he had a reputation for helping the community recruit new business. His Cannes townhouse on the French Riviera even appeared on television's "Lifestyles of the Rich and Famous."

Now he lives in Palm Beach and keeps his office a block off Worth Avenue but he keeps his operations considerably quieter these days. He is happily married for the last 10 years, to his wife Ingrid.

LaVergne, TN USA
09 March 2010
175332LV00001B/1/P